# SHAPING THE FIRST AMENDMENT

# The SAGE CommText Series

Editor:
**F. GERALD KLINE**
*Director, School of Journalism and Mass Communication*
*University of Minnesota*

**Associate Editor:**
**SUSAN H. EVANS**
*Annenberg School of Communications,*
*University of Southern California*

This new series of communication textbooks is designed to provide a modular approach to teaching in this rapidly changing area. The explosion of concepts, methodologies, levels of analysis, and philosophical perspectives has put heavy demands on teaching undergraduates and graduates alike; it is our intent to choose the most solidly argued of these to make them available for students and teachers. The addition of new titles in the COMMTEXT series as well as the presentation of new and diverse authors will be a continuing effort on our part to reflect change in this scholarly area.

—F.G.K. and S.H.E.

# John D. Stevens

# SHAPING THE FIRST AMENDMENT

## The Development of Free Expression

Volume 11. The Sage COMMTEXT Series

**SAGE** PUBLICATIONS
Beverly Hills / London / New Delhi

*For information address:*

SAGE Publications, Inc.
275 South Beverly Drive
Beverly Hills, California 90212

SAGE Publications India Pvt. Ltd.
C-236 Defence Colony
New Delhi 110 024, India

SAGE Publications Ltd
28 Banner Street
London EC1Y 8QE, England

Printed in the United States of America

**Library of Congress Cataloging in Publication Data**

Stevens, John D.
Shaping the First Amendment.

(The Sage commtext series ; v. 11)
Bibliography: p.
Includes index.
1. Freedom of speech—United States.
2. Freedom of the press—United States.
I. Title. II. Series.
KF4770.S83   1982         342.73'0853         82-10556
ISBN 0-8039-1876-3         347.302853
ISBN 0-8039-1877-1 (pbk.)

FIRST PRINTING

*For Gwen*

# CONTENTS

# ACKNOWLEDGMENTS

The intellectual debts are too many to begin to list; some are indicated in the references to the chapters. There is one mentor, however, who has to be mentioned specifically. That is Harold L. Nelson, who inspired me and a generation of graduate students at the University of Wisconsin to seek the linkages between law and history. Special thanks are extended to Diane Haft for her careful and speedy typing of the manuscript.

# INTRODUCTION

This book is an impressionistic sketch of trends in the development of First Amendment law and theory. Like a painting by Renoir or Monet, it tries to suggest rather than define. It suggests what free expression has meant in the United States and seeks to provide the reader with a basis for evaluating the continuing controversies that touch on the First Amendment. Like the viewer of an impressionistic painting, each reader must think through the implications in his or her own terms.

Most books on free expression are in a different tradition, one similar to that of painters such as Rembrandt or Wyeth, who insert the most minute details to represent reality. One style is not necessarily better than the other, for each must be evaluated on its own terms.

It is well at the outset to state some of the things this book is not. It is not a comprehensive survey of communication law, nor is it a handbook on how to avoid or defend against libel and privacy suits. It is neither a "case book," with long citations from court decisions, nor is it a legal treatise, with citations to every seminal book or decision.

The book is organized unconventionally. Chapters are not based on traditional divisions, such as broadcast regulation or obscenity; instead, the chapters focus on shared interest or experiences of persons or groups, regardless of what kind of law they sought to enact or under which they were prosecuted. For examples, chapters 4, 5 and 6 are quite unorthodox, focusing on ideologues, editors, and "protectors." These juxtapositions throw some fresh light on important issues.

There is a good bit of history in this book, more than in most books dealing with the First Amendment. For this the author makes no apology, for he firmly believes that the past is prologue.

Ann Arbor, Michigan                                    John D. Stevens

# 1

# THE PRAGMATIC VALUE
# OF FREE EXPRESSION

**Free expression is only one among many fundamental values in a free society. When, then, does it deserve a special place in that hierarchy? The answer is found not in ideology but in pragmatism. Without free expression, the other values mean little.**

Freedom to write, to speak out, to challenge—these are relatively recent concerns of mankind. For most of their existence on this planet, men and women have been too busy staying alive to worry about the need to express their innermost feelings. Even today, that freedom (even the concern about such freedom) is far from universal.

Since the time of primitive hunting packs, men have organized themselves into hierarchical structures, with all power gathered at the top. The principle has changed little through the centuries, although the societies became larger and more complex. Since in any authoritarian society all wisdom as well as power is at the top, it was logical for the communication systems to develop in one direction only, namely downward to carry decisions to those below who had no part in their formulation. Siebert et al. (1963) found this characteristic in all authoritarian societies, whether headed by monarchs, priests, or military dictators. For the ruler to permit dissent is an admission that he might not have a corner on all wisdom. Even when he asks for advice, he invites trouble.

The privilege of consultation can evolve into a genuine sharing of decision making, as it did in England, where beginning in the fourteenth century, a succession of monarchs conceded powers to Parliament in return for financial support for a long series of wars. When the Stuarts gained the throne, James I brought on a civil war when he tried to reassert the divine right of kings, as he did in this speech before Parliament in 1609:

> Kings are justly called gods, for that they exercise a manner or resemblance of divine power upon earth; for if you consider the

attributes to God, you shall see how they agree in the person of a king. . . . They make and unmake their subjects, they have power of raising or casting down, of life and of death, judges over all their subjects and in all causes and yet accountable to none but God only.

While this viewpoint has seldom been stated so nakedly in the modern world, it is implicit in all authoritarian societies. Its direct opposite is libertarianism.

## LIBERTARIAN THEORY

At its extreme, libertarianism means no controls on freedom. At its farthest extreme, it is anarchy. While no society has ever tried it to such extremes, it is useful as a theoretical construct. Defining rights as personal and absolute, libertarians recognize that there will be abuses but are willing to pay that price rather than have government set the boundaries. In the case of expression, they argue that to establish permissible limits would ultimately lead to a society unable to decide important questions for itself and thus easy prey for the demagogue.

The argument was given forceful form three centuries ago by John Milton in his *Areopagitica*. He wanted all ideas expressed because only in that way could true ideas win out over false ones. Although we are somewhat less sanguine about that in the light of twentieth-century history, all men want to believe it. It was the stuff of Aesop's fables five centuries before the Bible repeated the assurances about the meek inheriting the earth and about ultimate justice. The literature of all nations assumes some kind of just universe wherein the good are rewarded and the evil punished.

The writer most associated with the reasoning of a free marketplace of ideas is John Stuart Mill. This English philosopher set forth most of the arguments in his 1859 tract, *On Liberty*. The most often quoted sentences read:

If all mankind, minus one, were of one opinion, and only one person were of the contrary opinion, mankind would be no more justified in silencing that one person, than he, if he had the power, would be justified in silencing mankind. Were an opinion a personal possession of no value except to the owner; if to be obstructed in the enjoyment of it were simply a private injury, it would make some difference whether the injury was inflicted on a few persons or on many. But the peculiar evil of silencing the expression of an opinion is, that it is robbing the human race; posterity as well as the existing generation; those who dissent from the opinion, still more than those who hold it. If the opinion is right, they are deprived of the opportunity of exchanging error for truth; if wrong, they lose, what is almost as great a benefit, the clearer perception and livelier impression of truth, produced by its collision with error.

Notice that Mill's arguments are rooted in the *social* value of free expression. He sees expression as one right among many, one that must be balanced against the others.

Few seriously argue that expression must always take precedence over other values. Justice Hugo Black of the Supreme Court of the United States was often called an absolutist, but while he believed the Constitution permitted no limitations on written or spoken materials, he had little sympathy for so-called "symbolic speech." For Black, pickets and demonstrators use mob tactics and do not come under his brand of expression absolutism. On the other hand, Lyle Denniston (1981), a veteran newspaper reporter covering the Supreme Court, has argued for *no* restrictions. He would sooner tolerate the disclosure of defense secrets or the plotting of a political murder rather than have the government decide who could and could not express themselves and in what ways. It is not that Denniston advocates treachery or murder, for certainly he does not. But he argues that a society pays an even higher price if it allows its officials to ban speech, at the same time conceding that his logic could lead to anarchy. By spelling out the extreme implications of this doctrine of absolutism, Denniston serves an important purpose.

Of course, this is not necessarily to agree with him. Political science professor Samuel Krislov (1968) insists that absolutism, like any orthodoxy, can have a "paralyzing effect on thought itself—not just judicial thought, but also that of the general public." Absolutism promises more than it or any other ideology can deliver, namely "untrammeled discussion unfettered by time and circumstance." In the real world, judges are called upon to interpret any doctrine, and judges, both by temperament and training, are pragmatists. They are interested in what works far more than they are in ideological consistency. In philosophy, the term "pragmatism" is applied to the formulations of William James and others at the turn of the century, but its spirit is much older. It measures the truth of a proposition by its practical outcome. Truth is therefore a relative matter, subject to constant redefinition.

This book is firmly rooted in free expression as a pragmatic concept, not a theoretical one, however appealing the latter may seem.

## SOCIAL RESPONSIBILITY THEORY

The pragmatic view is inherent in the construct we call social responsibility. Unlike libertarian, absolutist, or authoritarian theory, this one sees free expression as a never-ending process, a search rather than a conclusion.

The theory emerged from deliberations of the Commission on Freedom of the Press in the years right after World War II. A panel of distinguished citizens spent many months evaluating the mass media of the United States. The final report of the nongovernmental body headed by Robert Maynard Hutchins, then chancellor of the University of Chicago, contains ideas that are as fresh today as they were in 1947. Their conclusions, although obviously reached within the American setting, are worth consideration by the citizens and governments of all free societies.

As one would expect, given the American situation, the commission favored private control of the media; however, it insisted that the managers either act responsibly or face the likelihood that they would be forced to do so through laws. Clean up your own acts, it said, or the government has not only a right but an obligation to do it for you. In its summary report (1947), the commission wrote:

> Freedom of the press means freedom from and freedom for. The press must be free from the menace of external compulsions from whatever source. To demand that it be free from pressures which might warp its utterance would be to demand that society should be empty of contending forces and beliefs. But persisting and distorting pressures—financial, popular, clerical, institutional—must be known and counterbalanced. The press must, if it is to be wholly free, know and overcome any biases incident to its own economic position, its concentration, and its pyramidal organization. The press must be free for the development of its own conceptions of service and achievement. It must be free for making its contribution to the maintenance and development of a free society. This implies that the press must also be accountable. It must be accountable to society for meeting the public need and for maintaining the rights of citizens

and the almost forgotten rights of speakers who have no press. It must know that its faults and errors have ceased to be private vagaries and have become public dangers. The voice of the press, as far as a drift toward monopoly tends to become exclusive in its wisdom and observation, deprives other voices of a hearing and the public of their contribution. Freedom of the press for the coming period can only continue as an accountable freedom. Its moral right will be conditioned on its acceptance of this accountability. Its legal right will stand unaltered as its moral duty is performed.

The drift toward monopoly is not a uniquely American phenomenon, of course; it has occurred throughout the world. More recently, many Canadians have been alarmed about the same thing. When two major newspapers went out of business on the same day, the Canadian government established a Royal Commission in 1980 to investigate monopoly ownership of the media. The commission easily documented that; in fact, it declared old-fashioned competition a thing of the past. Chains and conglomerates controlled Canadian newspapers, magazines, and a large share of the broadcast and cable outlets. While Parliament did not rush to enact into law the commission's recommendations about halting or even reversing monopoly ownership, the report (1981) provided a careful analysis of many problems, and much of its language was as applicable in other nations as in Canada:

> One of our witnesses who urged that we should recommend nothing, that the status quo is satisfactory, summarized his sentiment in the remark that the state has no place in the newsrooms of the nation. We agree. No one, no interest, has any place in the newsrooms of the nation except editors and reporters doing their professional job, to the best of their ability. The problem is that there is another presence: not the state, but outside business interest ... If the owners of newspapers have other business interest, the wells of truth are suspect. The presence in the newsroom is not normally visible. But it is there, the ghost at the party, and it sets an important part of the rules.

## PRAGMATISM OF COMMON LAW

It is idle to argue that there are never times when other rights must prevail over those of expression. The task for any society is to work out a way to resolve these conflicts as they arise. At least in the common law tradition of England and the United States, all decisions are couched in pragmatic terms.

Abraham (1968) found three characteristics that distinguish common law, and all three are strongly pragmatic. First, he said, is vitality and its ability to adopt to changed situations. Second is its refusal to assume that any rule is settled; instead, it is to be seen as a working hypothesis. Third is the moral obligation of those in society to live by the decisions of the courts.

Years before assuming his seat on the Supreme Court, Oliver Wendell Holmes, Jr. wrote in his classic book, *The Common Law* (1881):

> The life of law has not been logic; it has been experience. The felt necessities of the time, the prevalent moral and political theories, institutions of public policy, avowed or unconscious, even the prejudices which judges share with their fellow-men, have had a good deal more to do than syllogism in determining the rules by which men should be governed. . . . The very considerations which judges most rarely mention and always with an apology, are the secret root from which the law draws all the juices of life. I mean, of course, considerations of what is expedient for the community concerned.

Seldom has the case for pragmatism been put so directly or forcefully, but one judge who came close was Learned Hand (1953). He served with distinction for many years on the Second Court of Appeals and was perhaps the most venerated and quoted judge never to sit on the Supreme Court. He spelled out his views on the pragmatic nature of government and justice in his book:

> Jefferson is dead; time has disproved his forecasts; the society he strove to preserve is gone to chaos and black night, as much as the empire of Genghis Khan; what has succeeded he would disown as any get of his. . . . We shall not succeed by any attempt to put the old wine in new bottles; liberty is an essence so volatile that it will escape any vial however corked. It rests in the hearts of men, in the belief that knowledge is hard to get, that man must break through again and again the thin crust on which he walks, that the certainties of today may become the superstitions of tomorrow; that we have no warrant of assurance save by everlasting readiness to test and test again. William James was its great American apostle in modern times; we shall do well to remember him.

Media spokesmen will do well, too, to remember that freedom of expression is not theirs alone; rather, it is a societal right and belongs to all the people. When the media ask for favored legal status, they inevitably assume certain debts. Enough of those and they will find themselves unable to perform as they might like, for it is because of their performance that they have public support.

As Justice Felix Frankfurter wrote (Pennekamp v Florida, 328 U.S. 331, 1946): "The liberty of the press is no greater and no less than . . . the liberty of every citizen of the United States."

This puts the rationale for freedom of expression in the proper perspective. In a democratic society, the people need to be able to know and decide crucial issues for themselves. That, in a nutshell, is the pragmatic reason for granting a maximum of free expression. It is not to do the media a favor; it is to assure that the entire system works in the way we want it to.

# 2

## THE FREE EXPRESSION GUARANTEE

**The idea of free expression is an ancient one, but in its modern form it was hammered out in the Anglo-American tradition. The wording of the First Amendment mattered less than its spirit, and it took the Sedition Act crisis to give it recognizable form.**

There are only 45 words in the First Amendment to the Constitution of the United States, and none of them express radically new or different ideas:

> Congress shall make no law respecting an establishment of religion, or prohibiting the free exercise thereof; or abridging the freedom of speech, or of the press; or the right of the people peaceably to assemble, and to petition the Government for a redress of grievances.

The ideas, even some of the phrases, were drawn from existing sources and constitutions, and they were to be copied countless times by other nations. Their meaning—their strength—comes from the way they have been interpreted, both by the courts and, ultimately, by the public. This book focuses on just fourteen of those words: "Congress shall make no law . . . abridging the freedom of speech, or of the press." Religion, assembly, and even petition rights are interwoven, but they are not the central focus.

While it is a cliché to talk about "a living Constitution," no part of the Constitution has been more dynamic than those fourteen words dealing with free expression. Their limits have been shaped by the crises they have weathered. They will not mean the same thing ten, or even five years from now as they do today.

Governments tolerate dissent either when they lack the popular support to crack down or when they feel secure. The latter does not happen often. While our Constitution is a product of the late eighteenth-century Enlightenment, it drew on ideas far older than that.

## THE ANCIENT WORLD

The Greeks waited a long time before forcing Socrates to drink his hemlock. For years he had been challenging the basic assumptions of the society. In part this was because those in power—the educated elite—did not take the official religion seriously either, seeing it only as an opiate for the masses. Greek arts and literature flourished in that atmosphere of benign neglect.

When Socrates' most famous pupil, Plato, designed his utopian republic, there was no place for free expression. The all-wise, all-powerful despot would use information, children's stories, and the arts to further policies of the state.

Rome contributed little to the philosophy of free expression. In the later Roman Republic and the Early Empire, there were no legal restrictions on opinion. As in Greece, most of the leaders were nonbelievers in the state religion. Cicero, for example, defended a false religion as a political necessity for keeping the masses in line. The general policy in conquered areas was to blink at local religious cults, not wanting to rouse any needless opposition to the Roman governors. They clamped down only when powerful local groups demanded it. Pilate did not go out looking for Jesus. Even after the Romans outlawed Christianity, there were few prosecutions. The eventual crackdown coincided with the increasing political troubles of the Romans themselves. Like many governments to follow, they tried to focus all their problems—the very real problems of hostile neighbors and invaders—on a dissident local sect. Unfortunately for them, they had waited too long, and the sect was too powerful to put down (Bury, 1913).

By inventing the book, the Romans indirectly made a far greater contribution to the development of freedom, for this in turn made possible the codification of laws. Books, bound on one side and with numbered pages, made information retrieval far easier than did rolled scrolls. This was especially important in bringing together scattered legal references.

## THE MIDDLE AGES AND RENAISSANCE

While in both ancient Greece and Rome the rulers did not feel an obligation to prosecute those who questioned them, those in the Middle Ages did. The political goal was nation-building, and leaders of fragile alliances, busy consolidating duchies into states, did not want any divisive issues, especially religious ones. Consequently, they outlawed dissent.

When one starts from an assumption that religious dogma must be accepted as the literal word of God, compromise is impossible, for compromise with Truth is, by definition, Error. In this view, a heretic is not a human being and certainly not entitled to any rights. When questions of philosophy or religion get so narrowly defined, there can be no serious investigation in the arts or sciences, because on such frontiers of knowledge there are always questions that merge into philosophy. Each new discovery then has to be twisted to fit the existing ideology. It is the same method that modern ideologues of the right or the left impose on their intelligentsia, and the restrictions have the same stifling effect.

During the Renaissance, the focus of interest shifted slowly from salvation to things of this world. Other-worldliness was not abolished by decree; rather, human curiosity about man and his world was unleashed. The humanism of the fourteenth through sixteenth centuries freed the minds of men, and the arts flourished; however, it was in the seventeenth century that Galileo was forced to recant his "errors."

## GALILEO AND FREE INQUIRY

Although Galileo's problems occurred more than a century before the United States declared itself a nation, his experience is worth looking at in some detail for it illustrates, above all else, the futility of trying to keep free inquiry within official bounds.

For 2000 years, almost everyone had accepted the view that the earth was motionless and that it lay at the center of the universe. Upon this assumption had been built elaborate theories intertwining astronomy, philosophy, and theology. Copernicus called all this into serious question in 1543, suggesting that the sun, and not the earth, was the center of the universe. While brilliantly conceived and most suggestive, his book offered little real evidence for the theories that were published in the year of his death. Although the book was controversial, the Church did not ban it; rather, his suggestions were to be considered as constituting a hypothesis.

About a half-century after the Polish astronomer's death, a Dutch lensmaker invented the telescope. This permitted scientists to observe the celestial bodies, not just speculate about them. One of the most eager telescope users was Galileo, an Italian fascinated by all aspects of nature. Although he most certainly was aware of the Copernican theory, Galileo did not set out to prove or disprove it. As a devout Catholic, surely the last thing he set out to do was commit heresy or challenge papal authority. And yet he did both. Galileo saw through his telescope that, contrary to the accepted view, the moon was not a perfect marble that had been set in place for all time. To him, its peaks and valleys suggested change on the surface of the moon. The moons of Jupiter and of Mars certainly revolved around those planets, so why was it unthinkable that the earth might revolve around some larger celestial body? Galileo was not a retiring man, and he argued his conclusions loudly and publicly. Apparently, his manners offended as many Church officials as his ideas.

Church leaders insisted in 1616 that Galileo stop promoting as an established fact his idea that the sun was the center of the universe. For them, the disturbing Copernican notion was still an unproved speculation. Galileo bowed to their wishes, retired to his laboratory and observatory, and spent the next few years marshaling his evidence, which in 1632 he submitted as *Discourses* to the Vatican censor. No book on any topic could be published without that imprimatur. He never mentioned Copernicus or identified the theory, but the arguments coming from the mouths of his characters were unmistakable. The censor paused before hitting on a compromise. Galileo had to add a preface specifically denying that the book advocated Copernican ideas. Galileo agreed, but even the dullest scholar saw through the ruse. The censor was fired and Galileo was summoned before a clerical trial.

Why was the Church so outraged? Langford (1966) found two reasons. First, there was the matter of discipline. To allow Galileo to violate a direct order against publishing that the sun was the center of the universe was to condone his audacity and invite even more from others. Second, many clericals feared the unknown. To admit the possibility of a fundamental error might open the floodgates to other challenges to Church infallibility. They were comfortable with the older theology; they did not know the implications of the new.

Galileo was convicted and promised absolution if he would recant his errors. Contrary to much of the mythology, he never spent a night in a dungeon, nor was he seriously threatened with physical torture. He recanted willingly and apparently sincerely, insisting that he had misunderstood his earlier instructions and that he had never considered Copernicanism as more than a theory. That done, he returned to spend the last nine years of his life in his laboratory, and while he published important works on physics, he avoided astronomy.

His *Discourses* was published almost at once in countries beyond the power of the Vatican; however, it remained for nearly two centuries on the Church's index of forbidden books. It was removed only after scientific discoveries, notably Newton's laws of gravity, were applied to prove what Copernicus, and later Galileo, had suggested.

Galileo's story is often told to illustrate the inherent conflict between religion and science, a conflict Galileo never saw. Anticlerical writers have since used the high-handed (and clearly wrong) action of the Church in condemning a man for views that turned out to be correct as quintessential evidence of its venality. The case has been fictionalized into novels and plays in the same way that the 1925 Scopes "monkey trial" has been.

But Galileo is better seen as an example of the fiercely independent thinker, a zealot who believed in his cause with all his heart and who was determined to make others believe, too. Such men and women have provided the martyrs in all societies.

As Langford (1966) wrote:

> Galileo won the final victory, but with byproducts quite foreign to his intention. He would not have wanted his name to be used against the authority and infallibility of the Church. The one thing he probably did wish posterity to learn from his personal tragedy was that no new opinion is wrong simply because it is new. That lesson alone would be a worthy legacy.

## THE PRINTING PRESS AND PRIOR RESTRAINTS

Nothing contributed more to change than the invention of the printing press in the fifteenth century. In spite of efforts to control its output, the presses appeared with incredible speed throughout Europe and England within 50 years. From them poured a torrent of pamphlets, broadsides, and eventually newspapers that spread ideas (even heretical ones) far faster than the officials could control them. With the printing press, there was no longer a way to keep information from the masses, especially as literacy increased. The Church was undergoing massive changes anyway; now there were individual Bibles and tracts for people to read and study and—inevitably—to question. The Word no longer had to come through a church official. The temporal governments faced a similar challenge, because now their records were spread before a much larger audience. The press was, by definition, a watchdog, even if a tame one. At the same time, printing provided the government and the church with a powerful new tool to spread its own views and propaganda (Eisenstein, 1978).

The nature of controls changed with the arrival of the printing press. Now officials would attempt to censor material *before* it was disseminated, by insisting on advance approval to print. Until that time, punishments were imposed only for what had already been uttered. It was more efficient to halt a message before many copies of it were in circulation. Unfortunately, one never found them all.

It is worth differentiating the nature of prior and subsequent restraints. First, the penalties may be equally severe under either system, and the words or ideas punished may be precisely the same ones. Why, then, do theorists insist that prior restraints are so much worse? Perhaps Galileo's example will serve again. He had to submit his manuscript to a bureaucrat, who had to approve or reject it. It is always safer to say no, as that Church censor found out. Let us posit the same problem with a system of postpublication controls. Galileo publishes his tract, and the Church officials have not two, but three choices. They can give it their official blessing, they can prosecute him for what he has written, or they can ignore it. The third choice is not available to the prepublication censor.

There are philosophical as well as pragmatic reasons for preferring postpublication censorship. Most notable of these is that the ideas get a hearing, no matter how brief, before they can be suppressed.

Battles over freedom of the press centered for the next few centuries on eliminating prior restraints. Slowly, European nations removed such restrictions because they were both ineffective and unpopular. Many invented new controls that were equally effective. While this is not the place to recount such innovations, it is important to turn briefly to some of the developments in England, from which the United States inherited most of its traditions, including the legal ones.

## *ENGLISH ANTECEDENTS*

For an American interested in the English antecedents of freedom and its guarantees, the obvious place to begin is with the Magna Carta in 1215. In this document, English lords extracted written promises from the sovereign for the first time, rules that the king agreed not to violate. The concessions were made under duress, of course, and the lengthy enumeration (mostly on economic matters) includes not a word about human rights. There are no promises to respect what are now called civil rights; however, the document clearly displays a spirit that is important, namely the acceptance that there *are* basic rights, the most significant being trial by jury. The Magna Carta is not filled with memorable phrases, but its turgid and legalistic prose outlines the idea of inalienable rights for citizens. A major blow had been struck for human liberty.

During the turbulent sixteenth and seventeenth centuries, British monarchs invented all sorts of systems to check expression, ranging from outright licensing, to establishing guilds to police errant members, to enacting taxes on knowledge.

When Oliver Cromwell and his followers overthrew the king in 1649, they imposed even more severe restrictions than had the Tudors and the Stuarts. When they virtually eliminated the printing of news books, except for the official mouthpiece, handwritten newsletters carried by private couriers developed as an uncensored source of information for those who could afford such services. The period was punctuated by the publication of the first English newspaper in 1665, an official court publication.

In 1688 James II fled, and William and Mary assumed the throne on a promise of enacting a bill of rights, which was done the following year. It guaranteed freedom of debate in Parliament, habeas corpus, and some personal freedoms; however, there was no specific mention of freedom of the press. Through the centuries, habeas corpus has come to mean due process of law.

England was the first European nation to end prior censorship. This came in 1695, a half century after John Milton's brilliant treatise, *Areopagitica*. In it, the poet mustered just about every argument for the freedom to publish:

> Give me the liberty to know, to utter, and to argue freely according to conscience, above all liberties. . . . Though all the winds of doctrine were let loose to play upon the earth, so Truth be in the field, we do

injuriously, by licensing and prohibiting to misdoubt her strength.
Let her and Falsehood grapple; whoever knew Truth put to the worse
in free and open encounter?

Of course, Milton argued only for freedom of discussion for
serious-minded men on serious topics. He never urged such
freedom for lesser men or for lesser purposes. No one in his day did.

Since at least the time of John Milton, political speech has
enjoyed a special place in the pantheon of free expression
philosophy. It has been seen as the core; all else has been
peripheral.

Its principal modern American exponent was Alexander
Meiklejohn (1948) who urged absolute protection for speech or
writing that in any way contributes to the enlightenment of the
electorate. He thought the First Amendment would retain the most
power if its scope were limited to political speech. He was vague
about how much protection movies, stories, books, and speech
designed primarily for entertainment were entitled to. He seemed
to suggest that they were adequately protected by specific laws, but
that the First Amendment should be reserved for information about
government. The problem with his philosophy, a problem which
recent years have shown up even more clearly, is that the line
between political and other speech is not easily drawn. A political
idea may come wrapped in an obnoxious cover, either obscene or
presented by shouting or demonstrating.

Milton's treatise caused little stir in his own day. In fact, it was not
reprinted in a second edition until 1738. By then there were stirrings
for expanding freedom, and no place more so than in the American
colonies. On the road to the Revolution, Milton became one of the
most frequently cited authors in American newspapers, pamphlets,
and sermons.

Another Englishman, William Blackstone, set the terms of the
debate which would follow. An eminent jurist, his *Commentaries*
was the accepted authority on both sides of the Atlantic. Blackstone
defined freedom of speech as the absence of prior restraints. While
that was as far as he went, the rising revolutionary generation would
insist on more.


## THE EARLY AMERICAN EXPERIENCE

By 1791, when the First Amendment went into effect, Americans
had lived under various compacts and constitutions for nearly three

centuries. To attract ambitious settlers, land companies had granted greater personal and economic rights than were available at home. Even during periods when kings insisted on religious orthodoxy in the British Isles, they would wink at the way colonists in far-off North America worshiped. After all, their heresies could hurt no one except the Indians. This policy fostered more and more personal rights and local self-rule (Schofield, 1915).

The first printing press in the colonies arrived in 1638, and its Harvard University owners used it primarily for church printing, although it also turned out governmental forms. (Ironically, its very first product was a loyalty oath—hardly a harbinger of freedom.) The royal governors tried to keep tight reins on it and succeeding presses, but gradually the printers took on work for merchants, and there was a trickle of unapproved printing.

The history of each colony was different, but the pattern was essentially the same. There was some sort of popularly elected chamber, and through the decades this chamber gained more and more latitude at the expense of the royal governor and his cronies in the appointed upper chamber. Again, this was not by law but by custom. The idea was that the lower chamber would deal with day-to-day matters of local concern, but each year more and more affairs were so defined. When it took months for an exchange of correspondence between the governor and his supervisors back in London (complicated by unclear and overlapping jurisdictions), there simply had to be more decisions made locally.

The royal governor, as representative of the Crown, theoretically had despotic powers but in practice was seldom in a position to enforce high-handed orders, no matter how "legal" they were. The British were too interested in other parts of the world to be inclined to lend these governors the soldiers necessary to enforce unpopular rules.

As the printing presses inevitably spread to other colonies, the governors were less than pleased. For example, in 1671 the governor of Virginia wrote:

> I thank God we have not free schools nor printing; and I hope we shall not have these hundred years. For learning has brought disobedience and heresy and sects into the world; and printing has divulged them and libels against the government. God keep us from both!

Official opposition was only one reason that the presses did not spread faster in the colonies. The main reason was the lack of social and economic demand. There was a strong oral tradition among the common folk, many of whom were illiterate. They came from an England without a tradition of a mass press. Scribes served the colonial businessmen, clergymen, and governmental leaders quite adequately for several decades.

A Boston printer issued the first American newspaper in 1690, but it was halted after one issue because he had failed to obtain prior clearance. It was fourteen years before another printer tried a paper, and he was to have no competition for fifteen years—clear indications that there was little social or economic demand for newspapers. The second paper was a dull one, edited by a dull bureaucrat who steered clear of controversy and filled his paper with material copied from the months-old British papers.

## THE ZENGER TRIAL

Jurors, as well as legislators, felt their oats and sometimes ruled in ways totally inconsistent with the law as written. It would be difficult to find a better example than the celebrated trial of John Peter Zenger in New York in 1735 on a charge of seditious libel.

Seditious libel is almost impossible to define, but it has to do with bringing the government or its leaders into disrepute. By 1735, it had a long and odious history, having been used for centuries as a club to discipline printers (and before them, speakers) in England. Freedom from prior censorship was not involved in the Zenger trial. Zenger was being tried for material that had been printed in his New York *Weekly Journal*.

William Cosby had been governor of New York since 1732, and by most accounts he was a particularly obnoxious governor. At any rate, a group of businessmen wanted him replaced, and to further that end they financed Zenger to publish a series of satirical attacks on Cosby. There were only two newspapers in New York, and the other one operated as Cosby's mouthpiece. Apparently, Zenger did not write a word of the attacks; he was a printer, paid for his efforts, but since no name other than the printer's appeared on newspapers of the day, he was the one in official trouble.

Cosby probably overreacted, but then, such men usually do. Following a complex series of legal moves, he had Zenger charged and his attorney disbarred. Zenger's financial backers hired the best-known, most respected attorney in the colonies, Andrew Hamilton, who came in from Philadelphia. Hamilton needed all his famed eloquence, since the law required only one thing of the jury: to determine if Zenger was the publisher. Clearly he was, but Hamilton did what any attorney does when the law is against him: He argued what the law ought to be (Alexander, 1963).

Hamilton insisted that the English law had to be adjusted to American conditions. Since the essays had criticized the governor, and not the king, that same governor should not be allowed to determine if the words were injurious. Above all, Hamilton argued for two principles:

(1) the jury should be empowered to decide not only if the words were published but if they were offensive; and
(2) the truth should be a defense; in other words, the accused person should have a chance to prove in court that what he had said was factual.

Although the prosecution insisted that Hamilton was muddying the issues, the jurors took only a few minutes to acquit the printer. Perhaps the best indication that Zenger was a tool was that no one remembered to sign for his release from jail in time to attend the big celebration party that night.

Ironically, the Zenger case was apparently never used as a legal precedent. There simply are no other cases. Colonial governors read the writing on the wall and were not about to embarrass themselves by bringing hopeless prosecutions of those who attacked the government. The trial had great political repercussions on both sides of the Atlantic, becoming a rallying cry for defiance.

If antigovernment remarks could no longer be prosecuted successfully in the courtroom, they could be in the assemblies, and the popularly elected branches punished more printers and speakers than did the courts.

By the time of the Zenger trial, the six major colonial seaports all had their own newspapers, and there were competing papers in Boston, Philadelphia, and New York. Many thriving British cities with larger populations still had no newspapers at that time.

## THE AMERICAN REVOLUTION

The two dozen small weeklies in colonial America hardly looked like a threat to the British Empire a decade before the outbreak of fighting, but they became the tocsins of revolution. They did much to provide unofficial links among the colonies, exchanging copies and reprinting more and more about affairs elsewhere on the continent. It is important to remember that there were no official links among the colonies; each was tied by its own string to London (or, in the case of New York, to Holland).

Pamphlets and sermons were other forms of organized propaganda. Thomas Paine's *Common Sense* was published in early 1776, at the very moment the colonies were choosing their delegates for what was to become the congress declaring for independence. The 80-page pamphlet, unlike Milton's, caused an immediate stir.

Paine rejected every argument for continuing under the motherland. He mixed his calm, logical arguments with a liberal dose of demagogic, violently partisan rhetoric. First, he examined the British system and found little to praise. Then he considered the economic advantages to the colonies of remaining within the empire. Again, he found the advantages of a break far outnumbering the disadvantages, a view not shared by most American leaders at that point. Finally, he took the step that even the most virulent of the American leaders was wary of, directly denouncing King George III as a "Royal Brute." Paine called him the "greatest enemy this continent hath, or can have." It was a revolutionary message, and it closed with these ringing phrases: "There is something very absurd in supposing a continent to be perpetually governed by an island. In no instance has nature made the satellite larger than its primary planet."

*Common Sense* reportedly sold 120,000 copies in three months, and it was printed in whole or in part in many of the newspapers as well. Estimates are that eventually 500,000 copies were distributed; if so, it is the best selling book of all time, in relation to the American population, which at that time was only about 2.5 million.

Although many colonists feared a total break with England, that is what emerged from the summer meeting in Philadelphia. The Declaration of Independence, unlike almost any other announcement of political dissolution in the world's history, was phrased in measured, legalistic tones. It listed rights and grievances leading to the conclusion that the implied contract between the King and his subjects had been broken. There were no charges of bad faith. The British, of course, did not agree with the logic, nor did the colonists expect that they would. They were setting down their case "for the record."

The break with Great Britain that came in 1776 had been building for a long time. Each year, the American colonists became bolder in their defiance. They refused to buy taxed paper, threw tea overboard, and mob violence accompanied every stage up to the shooting at Lexington and Concord in 1775. The mob actions, according to Schlesinger (1955), highlighted grievances in ways mere words could not. Political riots were almost unknown in the colonies before the 1760s, although they were frequent in England. Some Tories were roughed up and a few tarred and feathered; however, there was not a single fatality in all the rioting.

British officials knew there was little point in prosecuting the rioters, because after the Zenger experience juries were not likely to convict.

Throughout the period, American leaders assumed they had all the rights of transplanted Englishmen plus others based on the uniqueness of their situation. Meanwhile, they paid fewer taxes and enjoyed more personal freedom than those in the homeland.

Merchants shifted their advertising and job printing from Tory to Patriot printers. So did the churches. Mobs became bolder in attacking Tory print shops. The Royal Mail Service was subverted by private couriers who served as conduits not only for routine mail, but for exchanging copies of newspapers and organized propaganda letters.

This is no place to recount the ensuing weary years of occasional battles. It was a war of attrition, the British hoping to put down the ragged American army with a minimum investment of troops while the Americans resorted to guerrilla warfare and waited for the unpopular war to take its toll in London. A large proportion of Englishmen saw the war as an endless stalemate, an expensive adventure, and aimed at persons with whom they shared much in tradition and culture. The eventual entry of the French tipped the scales.

American newspapers played up the rare victories and explained away the defeats, meanwhile devoting many columns to patriotic essays, including some by Paine. They faced shortages of ink, paper, and type, all of which had been imported but which infant native industries now strove to produce in sufficient quantity. The few Loyalist editors pulled up stakes when the British troops withdrew from their city. Quakers were dealt with as harshly for expressing pacifist views as were Tories for pro-British ones. The lands and fortunes of many Loyalists were confiscated and impounded, either by courts or by mobs. It is not a proud chapter in the history of freedom of expression, but genuine crises almost never are.

## RATIFYING THE CONSTITUTION

Until the final days of the two-month-long federal convention in 1787, there was little talk of including a Bill of Rights. That was not because the delegates doubted its importance, but rather that they were drawing up the blueprint of a government that would have no powers not specifically given to it. After all, eight states listed such rights in their constitutions, and there was no noticeable difference in the amount of freedom the citizens of those states enjoyed compared to the five states that did not list them.

The Constitution was sent to the states without such a Bill of Rights—a tactical error. There were those in each state who opposed the new Constitution for their own reasons (often because the central government had new powers over taxes and commerce), but they cloaked their opposition in terms of the dangers posed to personal freedoms.

Five states—Delaware, New Jersey, Pennsylvania, Georgia, and Connecticut—approved quickly. The first serious fight occurred in February 1788, when Massachusetts' convention approved it 187-168. Maryland, South Carolina, and New Hampshire ratified during the next four months, and with the approval of nine states, the Constitution went into effect. But four states still had not approved, and there was no hope of survival as a nation without both Virginia and New York. The battle for ratification settled on those two states, with James Madison leading one and Alexander Hamilton the other.

Several states conditioned their ratification on promises that the new congress would add certain amendments, many designed to protect individual rights. In the meantime, James Madison, Alexander Hamilton, and John Jay produced a series of brilliant essays on the nature of constitutional government. They were published anonymously in New York newspapers and then reprinted widely in other newspapers and pamphlets. Collectively, they were known as the *Federalist Papers*, and in number 84, Hamilton argued that laws could never protect personal liberties; only public opinion could do that. He thought such listings meaningless, but being a practical politician, he was willing to have the congress propose such amendments. His worry was that the demands would scuttle the whole Constitution, particularly in pivotal New York. He spoke for many when he asked: "For why declare that things shall not be done which there is no power to do?"

A far more cynical observer, the aristocratic Fisher Ames of Massachusetts helped adopt and send to the states the requested amendments, insisting they might do "some good towards quieting men who attend to sounds only." They were poppycock, of course, but they would make the rabble happy.

Both Virginia and New York approved the Constitution in the summer of 1789. In New York the margin was 89 to 79, and in Virginia it was 30 to 27. North Carolina and Rhode Island quickly added their ratifications.

At Madison's insistence, the new House of Representatives appointed a committee of eleven members—one from each of the states seated so far—to codify all the suggestions into amendments. The committee proposed twelve which, after some wording changes in the Senate, were submitted to the states. Ratification went smoothly for the ten dealing with human rights (two dealing with technical matters did not get enough votes to pass). The Bill of Rights went into effect in December 1791.

Farsighted though they were, the leaders could not possibly have envisioned what kind of nation they were founding or what its long-term needs might be. Theirs was a country of barely 3 million souls, clutching desperately to the edge of an inhospitable wilderness on one side and an equally inhospitable sea on the other. The 30 or so weekly newspapers published no more than 40,000 copies among them. They could hardly imagine a nation of 200 million, spread from coast to coast, and served by 60 million copies of daily newspapers and 200 million magazines a month; certainly, the idea of instantaneous communication via radio, television, and satellite was beyond their ken.

For them, "democracy" was not a term of approbation. It connoted "mobocracy," rule by temporary majorities in their own selfish interests. As students of world history, they knew that had often been the case. The excesses of the French Revolution were an example at hand. Jeffersonians, as they organized themselves into what we would call a political party, called themselves Republicans, not Democrats.

Writers on free expression have been fond of suggesting, without offering much evidence, that at the time of the adoption of the First Amendment, anyone with something to say could get a hearing. This may have been true for free white men with property, but even that is doubtful. At best, such a favored few might have been free to discuss, calmly and carefully, "serious issues." That usually meant politics, ethics, or religion, but even on those issues they usually had to watch themselves lest they go too far. Freedom was about where Milton had thought it should be in his own day, more than two centuries before.

This provides an important historical context for trying to divine what the framers "really meant" by the wording of the First Amendment. After an exhaustive study, Levy (1960) concluded that they agreed on only two things: freedom of expression meant the absence of prior restraints, and there was a crime of seditious libel. Although there was almost no disagreement on the first point, many wanted it to mean more than that. As for punishment for antigovernment sentiments, the question was seldom phrased so neatly. Often it was couched in terms of permissible freedom but dangerous license, the latter applying to words used by one's opponents. Certainly, the group known collectively as "the Framers" differed widely on where they would draw this line, but Levy insists that they all implicitly approved of punishment in some circumstances. Certainly Jefferson, as President, condoned "a few exemplary prosecutions" of his critics under New York's seditious libel law, even at a time when he felt the federal government had no such powers.

There were practical reasons to postpone the hammering out of a definition of freedom of expression. There were pressing problems, such as holding together a fragile coalition of states and keeping at bay the savage Indian tribes and the hungry nations that claimed the lands on all sides. The new nation had to get its commercial system functioning and its international trade and diplomatic ties established.

Pragmatic men that they were, the framers could not have thought they had settled much by adopting a Bill of Rights. They had erected a framework in which future generations could work out the applications in the light of changing circumstances; no one could reasonably have expected them to do more.

One of the most eloquent of all twentiety-century exponents of free expression, Zechariah Chafee, Jr. (1941), likened the First

Amendment to a barricade behind which journalists, authors, and speakers had a chance to pursue and present the truth. Chafee insisted that the barricade guaranteed nothing except the chance: "What the men inside the fence say when they are let alone is no concern of the law. It is, however, the concern of American citizens, and it ought to be the still greater concern of the men inside the fence."

There is more to free expression guarantees than the First Amendment, as Hans Linde (1981), an Oregon Supreme Court justice, has reminded us. There are also state constitutions and laws, as well as federal statutes that protect freedom of speech and of the press. Many of these are older and more expansive than the First Amendment itself. Theorists and lawyers alike almost forgot about these provisions after 1931, when the Supreme Court became involved, but as the Burger Court became less and less expansive, they were rediscovering them. Linde considered this a good thing and cautioned against too much reliance on the courts as protectors, since throughout most of American history the judicial branch has been the least libertarian.

Most of those who wrote about free expression at the time of the First Amendment's adoption—and there were not many—looked on procedural safeguards as the hope for freedom; however, the first real crisis would show how weak such procedural guarantees were. The test was not long in coming.

## THE SEDITION ACT OF 1798

As criminal laws go, it was not much. It was in effect for less than three years, and fewer than 20 persons were prosecuted under it. None of those who were convicted served more than a few months in jail for its violation, and yet the Sedition Act of 1798 provided the needed testing ground for defining free expression.

First, its context. During the summer of 1798, Congress passed a series of defense measures (raising a standing army, stocking arsenals, arming merchant vessels) in fear of an an invasion by the French. They also enacted internal security laws, the most notable being the Sedition Act, aimed at punishing critics of the government.

The threatened invasion never came, and the laws and their attendant tax bills helped sweep the Federalists out of office in 1801.

The high-handed and selective enforcement of the Sedition Act contributed to their electoral defeat.

The Federalists had controlled all branches of the federal government since its establishment, and they had come to equate their party with the government. There was no acceptance until decades later of the concept of parties alternating in office. Smith (1956) concluded that since most Federalists sided with the British, and since many Republicans expressed sympathy for the French Revolution as it swept across Europe, it was not difficult for the Federalists to see the Republicans as not only anti-Federalist but also anti-American.

From its passage that summer of 1978 until its expiration under its own terms on 3 March 1801, the day John Adams left and Thomas Jefferson entered the White House, the law was a blatantly partisan one. The Republicans in the House argued that the First Amendment barred restraints on expression, but predictably that argument failed, so with the key votes of a few Federalist members, they modified the law to include the very "protections" that had been argued for in the Zenger trial more than 60 years before.

The law provided up to two years in prison for publishing any "false, scandalous and malicious writing" against (1) the government; (2) either house of Congress, or (3) the president. The vice-president (who happened to be Thomas Jefferson) was *not* protected, and neither were federal judges. However, the judges wielded the contempt power in such a way as to need no extra protection, and Jefferson was the only Republican in the executive branch.

The protections represented the most liberal thought in the contemporary world. If a person was accused, he could defend himself by showing that either his motives were good or that what he said was true. The jury would decide if the words were criminal, not merely whether he was the person who had uttered them.

Jefferson and his followers were under no illusions. They knew the spirit of a witch hunt was in the air, and any doubts were eliminated quickly. The ink was hardly dry before the five leading Republican editors, among others, were indicted. Their papers were the sources for the political material copied by the smaller Republican newspapers throughout the land. The Federalists believed that by silencing them, they would silence them all. It was a misjudgment, for the indicted editors did not let up; in fact, they became more strident. They enjoyed publicizing the fifteen indictments under the law. All the victims were painted as martyrs. It was good campaign fodder, as were their ceaseless charges about bribery, frauds, doctored records, and incompetence by the incumbents.

Now let us turn to the trials. Every defendant was found guilty, in part because the judges were Federalists who interpreted the "safeguards" in such ways as to make them worse than no defenses at all, and in part because the grand juries and trial juries were overwhelmingly stacked with Federalists.

The truth defense was especially perverted. Smith found that the judges interpreted it to mean that the defendants had to prove the literal truth of every word and opinion, or in the words of one judge, "to the marrow." The same judge instructed a jury that if a defendant claimed three statements were true and could prove only two, then his defense failed. This reversed the normal presumption of innocence. He also told a jury that an editor's very attempt to prove the truth of his accusations demonstrated his bad intent.

Most of the trials took place during the spring of 1800, as the presidential campaign began shaping up. By the time Congress assembled in the new capital city on the Potomac late in the fall of 1800, it seemed likely the Republicans had captured the White House and both houses of Congress. The lame-duck Federalist Congress tried to extend the life of the Sedition Act for mixed reasons. Some Federalists argued that they wanted the "protection" of the law when they criticized the Republican incumbents; others wanted to expose themselves to the law to prove that there was nothing evil about it; and still others hoped to tempt Thomas Jefferson to make them into martyrs (Stevens, 1966). The efforts failed, and the law expired on the day the administrations changed. Jefferson pardoned all persons still imprisoned and canceled pending trials. Contrary to many secondary sources (including some Supreme Court dicta), the Republican-dominated Congresses during Jefferson's terms never made a general refund of fines to victims of the Sedition Act.

The act was so odious that the federal government did not pass another for 114 years; however, that did not stop the states from trying nor the federal government from narrowing the definition of free expression in more subtle ways.

Perhaps the best summary of the lesson of the Sedition Act experience comes from Henry Schofield, a noted constitutional authority. Schofield (1915) said it showed that "spokesmen of minorities may be terrorized and silenced when they are most needed by the community and most useful to it, and when they stand most in need of the protection of the law against a hostile, arrogant majority."

By the time Thomas Jefferson entered the White House, it was clear that Americans had not defined free expression merely by setting down the words in the First Amendment. Free expression meant more than those words, and it meant less than those words. The framers had not settled anything; they had merely provided a useful guideline. It would be up to each successive generation to protect its own freedom.

# 3

## WARS THAT SHAPED
## THE FIRST AMENDMENT

**Nothing reveals the nature of a society like a war. Its values are revealed by the legal and extralegal controls it places on aliens and dissenters.**

The first half of the nineteenth century was America's adolescence, and the remarkable, if jerky, growth in commerce, manufacturing, and population came with the awkward lurching of any teenager. After the War of 1812 (really a continuation of the Revolution), the British used their fleet to protect North America from other greedy nations and thus guarantee herself a commercial advantage. The result was that the United States enjoyed a long period in which it could concentrate almost entirely on its internal and commercial affairs.

Slowly, the sections of the new nation pulled apart. The Northeast's interests were in commerce and manufacturing, and the South's was in large-scale agriculture, which its leaders insisted depended on slave labor. The emerging Middle West found its interests with the Northeast, and the lines of commerce, transportation, and communication forged a political alliance between these two sections. The result is called, by many historians with 20-20 hindsight, "the irrepressible conflict."

### THE CIVIL WAR

All wars are brutal, but the most brutal are those that pit brother against brother. No war in American history did that like the Civil War. In retrospect, it is a wonder that civil liberties survived the five-year bloodbath as well as they did.

By the late 1830s (at a time the first newspapers for the masses were developing in the larger cities of the Northeast), the South had decided slavery was no longer a debatable issue. State laws punished any publication or talk that might conceivably incite slaves to insurrection. Georgia even made it a crime punishable by death. Soon the steam-powered printing presses in the border states were churning out Abolitionist tracts by the tens of thousands, and laws could not really halt their circulation. Congress specifically told the Post Office that it had no power to exclude such literature from the mails.

What laws could not do, mobs sometimes could. They ransacked Abolitionist print shops, lynching the editor in at least one case. Gradually, the mobs grew bolder, breaking up "disloyal" church services on both sides of the Mason-Dixon Line. With the actual outbreak of the war, some Northern colleges suspended any student who expressed the slightest understanding for the secessionist cause (Nelson, 1967).

The Civil War touched nearly everyone. It was the first war in which a sizable percentage of the population could read, and they devoured the newspapers for news of their loved ones. The emphasis shifted from opinion to news, and the reporter came into his own. His efforts were aided immensely by the use of the telegraph, although the reporter could use the facility only when the military had no need for it. This kind of informal censorship did more than the limited legal controls to shape the news that citizens read.

Newspaper editors in both the North and the South led cheers for the war, and when they were not enthusiastic enough to satisfy local sentiment, they were sometimes visited by vigilantes. There were at least 60 documented attacks on print shops in the North and probably as many in the South. Once, a mob refused to disperse until James Gordon Bennett agreed to hang a Union flag in the window of his New York *Herald*, by then the largest circulation newspaper in the nation.

When Union generals shut down some newspapers for printing news of troop movements, news that clearly might be of value to the enemy, Lincoln revoked the orders. Although these and similar newspapers had been lambasting him and his policies mercilessly, the President said their suppression "was likely to do more harm than the publication would do."

A military commission in 1862 convicted the editor of the Boone County (Missouri) *Standard* of encouraging resistance to the government and laws of the United States. His printing equipment was seized and he was ordered out of the state for the rest of the war.

Although neither side passed an effective sedition law, many newspapers were halted under the broader war powers. To his lasting discredit, Lincoln suspended the writ of habeas corpus, and before the Supreme Court could declare his action unconstitutional, thousands of civilians were jailed and some tried by military authorities for unpatriotic speeches or writing. The Confederate congress suspended the writ three times for short periods during the war. Neither Abraham Lincoln nor Jefferson Davis ordered any of these arrests, but they permitted them all.

The noted constitutional authority, Zechariah Chafee, Jr. (1941), while not excusing these excesses of enforcement, pointed out that at least Lincoln (and Davis, too) proceeded only against those persons who were "so far within the test of direct and dangerous interference with the war that they were actually causing desertions." In future wars, the net would be spread more widely.

The strictness of censorship on war correspondents varied with the general and how the war was going. Some hated all journalists, while others did their best to house, feed, and transport them, as well as allow them access to courier and telegraph services. When they were suffering reverses, the generals were likely to blame the newspapers for lowering morale or giving away secrets. Journalists have always been convenient scapegoats.

In 1866 the Supreme Court declared the war power of Congress to be restricted by the Bill of Rights. The case (Ex Parte Milligan 4 Wallace, U.S. 2) involved the trial of an Indiana editor by an army tribunal. The editor was accused of publishing pro-Southern propaganda and of actually plotting an action against the United States government; thus, it was not a *pure* speech case. The Supreme Court did not consider First Amendment aspects, but instead decided that a civilian should not have been tried by the military in an area where the civilian courts were functioning. The court ruled that civil courts must decide if the judicial machinery was adequate; otherwise, it would allow the military in any war, regardless how small or distant, to put the country under military dictatorship.

Also on the positive side, few repressive laws were enacted that could later be reinstated during another crisis. And the courts and legislatures did renounce many of the excesses, a not insignificant advance.

In the years immediately following the war, the First Amendment had little real meaning for those living in the former Confederate states. During the so-called Reconstruction Era, these areas were governed by military commanders and the laws were enforced by Union soldiers, still smoldering in their wartime animosities. There was little real freedom of the press in such a setting.

The Spanish-American War, which ended the nineteenth century with an exclamation point, raised few issues of censorship or suppression. Indeed, many citizens believed that the New York papers were all too free in their fanning the flames of war. As in the Civil War, relations between reporters and commanders varied, but since it was such an easy and quick campaign, it was for the press "a splendid little war." Never again would the correspondent enjoy such an enviable position: close contact with the commanders and the combat without the burdens of "instant communication" that technology would place on him. Both the commanders and the editors at home would keep a closer check on correspondents in the future (Knightly, 1975).

For all their excesses, it was the newspapers and magazines that revealed gross incompetence and chicanery by government officials who bought "embalmed beef" and woolen clothing for soldiers in the tropics. Medical care was scandalous. A few reporters also reported the long, bloody, and often-forgotten aftermath of the war—the Philippine Insurrection—which waged on for years with attendant brutalities and excesses.

Some American reporters covered the later border hostilities with Mexico and General Pershing's long pursuit of the guerrilla, Pancho Villa. But this was a ripple that preceded the tidal wave we call World War I.

## WORLD WAR I AND ITS AFTERMATH

On the night before he was to go before Congress to request a declaration of war on Germany, President Wilson is reported to have told one of his favorite journalists: "Once lead this people into war and they'll forget there ever was such a thing as tolerance. . . . The spirit of ruthless brutality will enter the very fibre of our national life."

The prediction was all too accurate. In no other American crisis, before or since, were civil liberties so trampled. Thousands— perhaps tens of thousands—of persons were prosecuted under laws or by vigilantes for uttering remarks that some of their neighbors found "antiwar." While many of the victims were German-

Americans, religious pacifists, labor radicals, and socialists, no one was safe. The fear that raged through the land during the 20 months of America's formal participation in the "war to end all wars" left an ugly scar, both on our traditions and in our statute books and court opinions.

When in April 1917, the United States entered the war, Americans had been watching from the sidelines for nearly three years. It was not the press that led the country into the war; in fact, studies showed leading American newspapers consistently trailed public opinion for entering on the side of the Allies. Neutral shipping rights might be abstract, but the loss of American ships and lives to German submarines was not.

America, unshackled from the pretense of neutrality at last, reacted in some ways that were humorous (renaming sauerkraut "liberty cabbage," dachshunds "liberty pups," and "German measles "liberty measles," for example). But it is hard to find much humor in the lynching of an Illinois man who refused to buy enough bonds or in the hundreds of incidents where mobs either tarred and feathered or poured yellow paint over suspected "slackers." To make matters worse, some of these "patriots" carried official-looking badges, issued to them as unpaid volunteered investigators for the Justice Department. It is even more disturbing to find that the federal, state, and local lawmakers enacted all kinds of restrictive legislation and that the courts (and juries) used the laws in the broadest possible ways (Murphy, 1979).

Why the strong reaction? American society had been built on the myth of homogeneity. No matter where a person came from, went the myth, he or she magically became an "American" here, leaving behind any nationalistic loyalties. That there was little evidence to support this myth only increased the tenacity with which Americans clung to it. The Civil War had not tested the myth, since it was an internal, "family" blood-letting, and the Spanish-American War had not tested much of anything, either. America, through the quirks of history and the British fleet, had been able to do what almost no other major power had ever been able to do: avoid major foreign entanglements. Rather than explaining this as an accident of history, Americans swelled out their chests and took full credit, convinced the United States was unique. Woe unto anyone who dared to question Manifest Destiny! It was a shock to the majority of Americans to find that from 1914 on, a sizable minority of their fellow citizens were disagreeing on foreign policy.

And so it was war, and not just an ordinary war, but a holy war to rid the world of the "Hun" and all his traces. Such a war does not begin or end at the water's edge. The 1910 Census listed 2.5 million Americans as "German-born" and more than twice that many who had at least one parent born in Germany. Millions spoke German in their homes; in fact, there was a well-established German subculture in the United States complete with its own theaters, businesses, schools, and newspapers. Like other immigrants, Germans tended to gather in ethnic enclaves, with the early settlers serving as magnets for newcomers. Until the war, the Germans had been among the most respected and popular of all immigrant groups. The fury that suddenly broke upon them represented what Higham (1955) called "the most spectacular reversal of judgment in the history of American nativism." Libraries burned German-language books, symphonies removed all German compositions from their repertoires, schools stopped teaching German, and universities fired professors of German. The federal government clamped down on German-language newspapers. By the thousands, citizens, banks, businesses, and even towns lined up to anglicize their names.

Vigilantes took it upon themselves to demolish a five-foot metal statue that adorned the second story of a downtown building in Green Bay, Wisconsin. Early one morning they looped a stout rope around the "symbol of German Kultur" and pulled it down. The crash was so loud that a man in a nearby all-night diner thought it was a "Kaiser bomb" for sure. The perpetrators scattered, but they must have been chagrined a few hours later when the owner of the building explained that what they had smashed was the figure of the Goddess of Liberty. The incident could serve as a metaphor for the entire period.

Americans have always been peculiarly susceptible to the delusion that another law or two will cure any ill of society. Therefore, it is not surprising that they turned to their lawmakers for cures in 1917. Congress enacted a draft, many restrictions on aliens, and established a propaganda bureau, but three federal laws are worth a detailed look: the Threats Against the President, Espionage, and Trading-with-the-Enemy Acts.

The nation entered the war with only the Conspiracies Act and the Treason Act from the Civil War, neither of which applied to individuals who uttered disloyal remarks. Although a handful of anarchists were convicted under the Treason Act, both of the laws involved conspiracies, a much more difficult standard of legal proof. Congress quickly corrected that deficiency.

There had been suggestions for a law to protect the president from threats since the assassination of McKinley two decades earlier, but it was not until early 1917 that Congress enacted one. It provided five years for making "any threat to take the life or to inflict bodily harm" upon the president. Federal judges interpreted "threats" so broadly as to be akin to the fifteenth-century English high treason law that made it a crime to *imagine* the death of a sovereign. By June 1918, 35 persons were convicted, and twice that number indicted. One was a young farmer who went to federal prison for a year for saying that if he had an airplane (which he certainly did not, and if he had one, he could not fly), he would fly over the White House and "get that damned Wilson." Another man said (three weeks after the Armistice): "I will shoot Wilson, the son of a bitch, if the country goes dry July 1." He pleaded guilty and got off with a 30-day sentence. Neither individual seemed to pose much threat to the President.

If, as Roche (1963) has suggested, World War I was a "black mass celebrated by the elected leaders of the American nation," then surely the Espionage Act was its litany. Only two provisions of the lengthy law affected free expression. A section of Title I made it a crime punishable by up to 20 years in prison to interfere with the military or recruiting services, and Title XII made it illegal to mail matter that violated other sections of the law. Strictly construed, these would have posed little threat to expression. That they were not so construed was shown by the number of prosecutions. Chafee (1941) wrote that 877 persons were convicted and more than 100 publications banned from the mails under the law. He based his estimates on annual reports by the Attorney General, but the author's detailed study of one state showed Chafee's figures to be extremely low. At least 2000 persons were indicted under the Espionage Act, almost all of them for what they said or wrote (Stevens, 1969).

The press did not see the law as a threat to expression; indeed, they congratulated themselves on stripping from the bill a formal censorship provision. Even when it became clear that federal prosecutors and judges were giving the law the widest possible interpretation, few publications cried out; instead, many called for military trials and even the death penalty. Meanwhile, the states fell over one another outlawing and punishing almost exactly the same offenses covered by the federal law. Punishments were harsh. At least 35 persons received the maximum 20-year sentence under the federal law. (Two states, not to be outdone, set their maximum at 21 years.) After the war, the man who had directed the Justice Department's efforts admitted that the laws caught only petty violators and not a single saboteur.

Of the 92 indictments in Wisconsin, for example, all but two were for expression. Many were indicted for praising Germany or the Kaiser, remarks more likely to provoke a punch in the nose than a danger to national security. For example, one farmer was accused by his neighbor of expressing doubts about alleged German atrocities (which postwar investigations would show were almost totally fake). The neighbor's testimony was accepted, even though he admitted a long-standing grudge with the accused. Although the accused farmer (whose son was serving in France at the time) denied the accusation, it took the jury only 35 minutes to convict him, send him to prison for a year, and fine him $1000 (Stevens, 1969).

Many other indictments were for criticizing the war effort (even for suggesting that it was not strong enough) or the Allies. There were even indictments for suggesting that the Red Cross or the YMCA did not deliver all the services to soldiers that they had promised. Many indictments quoted the shibboleth, "It's a rich man's war, but a poor man's fight." In Germany, socialists were being prosecuted for the same remark. The postmaster of a small Wisconsin town got into trouble for questioning the constitutionality of the Espionage Act itself.

Although the 1918 amendment added a new wrinkle to American law by protecting symbols from offensive words (military uniforms, Liberty Bonds, the Constitution, and the flag), most juries were convicting for those remarks from the start. The amendment had little practical effect.

On a hot Saturday in August 1918, there was great excitement in the little town of Corliss, Wisconsin. Men and women were scurrying about, stringing up bunting and flags for a Red Cross parade. The town marshal was stepping back to admire the decorations, when he saw a threshing rig heading straight for the biggest American flag, draped from a wire across the main street.

Apparently, the rig operator did not hear the warnings. Suddenly, the top of his steam machine caught the flag, yanked it down, and devoured it.

Men raced out and waved down the operator, who pulled over to the side of the road. Over the incessant roar of the machine, they carried on an animated conversation.

"Keep the damned flag out of the road," the operator shouted. "It's a public highway."

The operator was indicted for insulting the flag, not for tearing it down, but for calling it a "damned flag." He pleaded guilty and got off with a fine.

The Trading Act dealt mostly with commercial matters, but moments before passage, the Senate added a rider requiring all foreign-language publications to file with their local postmasters literal translations of all articles dealing in any way with the war. The added costs and hassle caused many small newspapers to close up shop, while others switched to English. Others tried, with mixed success, to avoid war issues entirely.

A crotchety old man edited the little Eau Claire (Wisconsin) *Herold.* In one issue, he published a long, barely coherent editorial criticizing the army's requirement that all recruits receive smallpox vaccinations, and since he filed no translation, he was indicted under both the Trading and the Espionage Acts. At his trial, his son and others testified that the old man was senile and did not really understand the translation requirement. Further, they said, he was harmless enough and his paper was only read by a handful of his cronies, anyway. They begged the judge to show mercy. His version of mercy was a year in Leavenworth, where the old editor died.

Across the state, another editor of a German-language weekly was indicted for not filing a translation of an editorial stating that he would not comment on war issues and citing the Eau Claire editor's plight to justify his policy. That commentary was interpreted as touching on the war and therefore requiring a translation.

The registration and draft went much more smoothly in World War I than officials expected, certainly better than it had during the riot-ridden Civil War. The Selective Service Act of 1917 required each draft-age man to carry either a registration certificate or classification card. During March 1918, some nine months after the initial draft sign-up of 10 million men, the Justice Department organized a series of "slacker raids." Operatives swooped down on theaters, street cars, restaurants, ball parks, pool rooms, and other public places. Any man unable to produce a card was hauled off to a police station or an armory. In New York City alone, an estimated 75,000 were arrested and spent at least one night in a makeshift jail, although it turned out that fewer than 3 percent had actually not registered; the others simply did not have their cards on their person. In the ensuing outrage, President Wilson ordered an inquiry and Congress condemned the raids. They were not repeated.

There were striking differences in the way the laws were enforced in different parts of the country. In Massachusetts, for example, the District Attorney refused to bring any cases, and while the Bay State had more than its share of military posts, ports of embarkation, and war plants (plus a large alien population), it experienced no more sedition or sabotage than anywhere else. Enforcement was strictest in the Upper Midwest, the Plains States, and the Pacific Northwest, all areas that had known radical and union unrest before and during the war.

Postmaster General Albert Burleson was ruthless. He ordered local postmasters to forward to Washington all publications that appeared to be "antiwar." He would then decide whether to issue show-cause orders to the submitters on why they should not lose their highly advantageous second-class mailing permits. Few could make the showing and were thus forced either to pay the higher rates or to cease publishing. He later interpreted the law so as to give postal officials the right not to deliver mail to addresses of those considered suspicious. This put crimps on fund-raising efforts by small dissident groups.

No World War I law—federal or state—was found uncon-stitutional by the courts. In spite of the Supreme Court's admonition in the Milligan decision in the Civil War (that war powers are not unlimited), the courts are generally reluctant to second-guess military leaders, including the president as commander-in-chief.

There were some unreasonable interpretations of the World War I laws. Although in most crimes courts require proof of injury, a nationwide study of the wartime prosecutions found no federal prosecutor who even attempted to prove that words had interfered with military recruitment. Juries never had a chance to consider how much danger certain words posed to security. It was enough to show that they had been uttered.

During the next half-dozen years, the Supreme Court decided a series of cases arising out of convictions under the wartime laws. It is important to remember that it had done this only a few times before, and then only in isolated cases. It never reviewed a case under the Sedition Act of 1798 nor, except for the Milligan decision (which turned on court jurisdiction rather than on free expression), under Civil War expression limits. The dearth of expression on cases is not difficult to explain. The federal government seldom had enacted such limits, and the Court had not yet asserted its right to review state attempts to do so.

It was in the first of these World War I cases, Schenck v. United States (249 U.S. 47), that Justice Oliver Wendell Holmes set down his landmark "clear and present danger" test, a test which had been cited by jurists in various contexts ever since. Schenck was convicted under the Espionage Act for circulating a leaflet that called on the public to resist the conscription law. Although the flyer was vague on exactly how this opposition should be expressed, Holmes reasoned that those who circulated it must have intended, at least, that those of draft age should refuse to serve in the army.

Holmes, who was intensely proud of his own Civil War military record, wrote:

But it is said, suppose that that was the tendency of this circular, it is protected by the First Amendment to the Constitution. Two of the strongest expressions are said to be quoted respectively from well-known public men. It well may be that the prohibition of laws abridging the freedom of speech is not confined to previous restraints, although to prevent them may have been the main purpose. We admit that in many places and in ordinary times the defendants in saying all that was said in the circular would have been within their constitutional rights. But the character of every act depends upon the circumstances in which it is done. The most stringent protection of free speech would not protect a man in falsely shouting fire in a theatre and causing a panic. It does not even protect a man from an injunction against uttering words that may have all the effect of force. The question in every case is whether the words used are used in such circumstances and are of such a nature as to create a clear and present danger that they will bring about the substantive evils that Congress has a right to prevent. It is a question of proximity and degree. When a nation is at war many things that might be said in time of peace are such a hindrance to its effort that their utterance will not be endured so long as men fight and that no Court could regard them

as protected by any constitutional right. It seems to be admitted that
if an actual obstruction of the recruiting service were proved, liability
for words that produced that effect might be enforced. The statute of
1917 in § 4 punishes conspiracies to obstruct as well as actual
obstruction. If the act, (speaking, or circulating a paper), its tendency
and the intent with which it is done are the same, we perceive no
ground for saying that success alone warrants making the act a crime.

Later in the same term, Holmes used his clear-and-present-
danger test to vote against upholding a conviction; however, the
court majority used the same test to convict. Abrams was convicted
under the Espionage Act for tossing from the upper stories of a New
York City building flyers in both English and Yiddish that criticized
the American government for dispatching troops to Russia, surely
one of the most bizarre sideshows of the war. The pamphlet ended
with this P.S.: "It is absurd to call us pro-German. We hate and
despise German militarism more than do your hypocritical tyrants.
We have more reasons for denouncing German militarism than has
the coward of the United States."

Holmes could not see how this pamphlet's distribution harmed
the American war effort. We were not at war with Russia, and even
the court's majority recognized that Abrams's primary intent was to
aid Russia.

Chafee (1941) said: "The decision of the majority worked
injustice to the defendants, but its effect on the national ideal of
freedom of speech should be temporary in view of its meager
discussion and the enduring qualities of the reasoning of Justice
Holmes." Indeed, this paragraph from the Abrams dissent (250 U.S.
616) is one of Holmes's lasting monuments:

Persecution for the expression of opinions seems to me perfectly
logical. If you have no doubt of your premises or your power and
want a certain result with all your heart you naturally express your
wishes in law and sweep away all opposition. To allow opposition by
speech seems to indicate that you think the speech impotent, as
when a man says that he has squared the circle, or that you do not
care wholeheartedly for the result, or that you doubt either your
power or your premises. But when men have realized that time has
upset many fighting faiths, they may come to believe even more than
they believe the very foundations of their own conduct that the

ultimate good desired is better reached by free trade in ideas—that the best test of truth is the power of the thought to get itself accepted in the competition of the market, and that truth is the only ground upon which their wishes safely can be carried out. That at any rate is the theory of our Constitution. It is an experiment, as all life is an experiment. Every year if not every day we have to wager our salvation upon some prophecy based upon imperfect knowledge. While that experiment is part of our system I think that we should be eternally vigilant against attempts to check the expression of opinions that we loathe and believe to be fraught with death, unless they so imminently threaten immediate interference with the lawful and pressing purposes of the law that an immediate check is required to save the country. . . . Only the emergency that makes it immediately dangerous to leave the correction of evil counsels to time warrants making any exception to the sweeping command, "Congress shall make no law abridging the freedom of speech." Of course I am speaking only of expressions of opinion and exhortations, which were all that were uttered here, but I regret that I cannot put into more impressive words my belief that in their conviction upon this indictment the defendants were deprived of their rights under the Constitution of the United States.

While the court reversed no convictions under the wartime laws, in upholding the conviction of a socialist convicted under the New York statute, it took the giant step of applying First Amendment standards to the states. Benjamin Gitlow was convicted of publishing a left-wing manifesto so tedious that not many could ever have read it. (Gitlow was a major figure in the byzantine maneuverings of the left for decades, ending up as a professional anticommunist informant for congressional committees in the 1950s.) The important point is not that the Supreme Court upheld his conviction under New York law, but rather that they reviewed it at all.

The court asserted that it had jurisdiction because under the Fourteenth Amendment, states could not "deprive any person of . . . liberty . . . without due process of law." It said that unreasonable or arbitrary limits on speech constituted such a deprivation. Case by case over the next several years, the court found more and more forms of expression thus protected from state limitations, until today it is safe to say that if the federal government can't regulate the expression, neither can the states. This was a gigantic step because until 1925, the Supreme Court had refused to review such state laws, and it was the states that usually limited expression.

Freedom of the press and of speech had been accepted slogans for a long time, but they were defined in this series of World War I cases. The new definition moved in two directions. The first is the one just discussed, namely that the states as well as the federal government were obligated to respect expression. The second was to see freedom of expression as a public issue—especially when it touched on political issues—not primarily as a private property right to be protected by civil actions for libel and related matters. Expression was on the public agenda to stay.


## WORLD WAR II AND ITS AFTERMATH

Realistically, the United States was not imperiled in 1917. It entered that war to aid its traditional friends and to maintain the world's geopolitical balance. In 1941 the nation was attacked, its fleet crippled, and its own shores threatened by bombs or even invasion. This global, life-or-death struggle lasted more than twice as long and claimed more than three times as many Americans dead and wounded as had World War I.

At home, however, the mood was calm. Neither prosecutors nor mobs hounded those who uttered idle criticisms of the war effort. Although the Espionage Act was in force, there was a grand total of one prosecution. There was no censorship of the press, not even the foreign-language press. Aside from a handful of the most virulent fascist publications, the mails were not closed to critics of the war. With the exception of the incarceration of 110,000 Americans of Japanese ancestry—a tragic blunder made the more so by the Supreme Court's holding in Korematsu v. United States (323 U.S. 214, 1944) that it was constitutional—the civil liberty record during World War II was infinitely better than in World War I. Why?

First, those in the Roosevelt administration had learned from earlier wars and were determined not to repeat any excesses. The Attorney General ruled that no Espionage Act prosecution could begin until he personally had approved it. Similarly, the Postmaster

General kept tight reins to make sure his inspectors did not go too far in "cleansing" the mails of disloyal matter. In Congress, when censorship of the foreign-language press was proposed, several members rose to recite the sorry experience of World War I, and it was not enacted.

The courts were much better equipped (and much more willing) to protect civil liberties, too. The Supreme Court's treatment of the 1920s war cases provided a rationale for tolerating dissent, as did a series of 1930s decisions upholding the rights of religious groups to distribute their information and for labor unions to organize and demonstrate.

With the exception of the Japanese (see Chapter 6, this volume), alien groups did not seem to pose much of a problem to most citizens. Since large-scale immigration had ended in the 1920s, even the leaders of most of the nationality groups were second- or third-generation Americans, unable even to speak their native languages. American propaganda trumpeted the "one-nation" message, and it was difficult for racists to advocate policies in harmony with those of the Third Reich. The federal government prosecuted the leaders of the handful of tiny fascist groups, and that helped quell the fears of the average American, who turned his energy to winning the war rather than waging a homefront crusade.

In 1917 the Committee on Public Information was in charge of both war information and voluntary press censorship. There were times when those two roles were in conflict, so in 1941 these functions were placed under separate offices, each headed by a journalist of national respect. Radio had become a major concern in the interim and required much more attention. In spite of its voluntary nature in both wars, there were almost no violations of censorship guidelines.

What kinds of material were listed as sensitive? Production figures from war-related industries or hints of troop movements or concentrations were the main topics, but radio stations could not broadcast weather reports or live interviews on the street for fear of using codes to convey sensitive information. One serious breach was when the Chicago *Tribune* published a story revealing that the United States had broken the Japanese code and was gaining valuable information by monitoring the enemy broadcasts, but the paper was not prosecuted for its error.

There were a few trials for treason during World War II. Treason is carefully defined in Article III of the Constitution:

> Treason against the United States shall consist only in levying War against them, or in adhering to their Enemies, giving them Aid and Comfort. No Person shall be convicted of Treason unless on the Testimony of two Witnesses to the same overt Act, or on Confession in open Court.

Courts have always insisted that talk, plans, schemes, or hopes are not enough; treason requires overt acts. Usually those who have been accused have been far within the definition; however, some World War II cases raise an issue.

Several American citizens were accused of treason for making broadcasts from enemy territory and under enemy government sponsorship aimed at lowering the morale of American fighting men. Although defense attorneys tried to argue that this was protected speech, the courts insisted that speech used as a deliberate part of the enemy effort was unprotected.

The Alien Registration Act of 1940 (commonly called the Smith Act) was first used in 1943 against 18 members of the Socialist Workers Party, but it was not enforced again until the postwar anti-communist hysteria. (see Chapter 6, this volume).

## THE WAR IN VIETNAM

American participation in the UN "police action" in Korea in the early 1950s produced little protest at home. Vietnam, however, was another matter. It was not only the longest but probably the most frustrating war in American history. For the first time, citizens saw a war in all its horror on their television sets, and as their frustration mounted, they liked less and less what they saw and read.

When President Johnson started sending combat troops to Vietnam in 1965, three-fourths of all Americans supported the escalation. Until then, U.S. military personnel had been only advisors in Vietnam. Three years later, at the time of the Tet Offensive, a majority of the American public admitted to pollsters that they were fed up with the war. They were dismayed by antiwar protests and demonstrations at home and with casualties and deaths on the battlefield.

Never before had the courts and the public tolerated such strident protest. From the White House on down, there was an assumption that however wrong they might be, protesters had a right to march, shout, write, and demonstrate, even in the most shrill manner. The much-publicized trials should not obscure how few there were. An even better gauge of public toleration is the almost total lack of vigilante or mob action against protestors. That, too, was new.

The most liberal definition ever of grounds for conscientious objection was hammered out (see Chapter 4, this volume). There were even overtures of forgiveness to those who fled to Canada and other countries to avoid the draft. Such actions would have been unthinkable in earlier wars.

In 1969 the Supreme Court reversed a conviction of a young black who told an antiwar rally: "If they make me carry a rifle, the first man I want to get into my sights is LBJ." One shudders to think of his chances before a court in 1917 or 1918, but in Watts v. U.S. (394 U.S. 705) the court ruled that this was "political hyperbole" directed at the society rather than the President personally.

Protests became commonplace. Some received much attention, such as the 1967 March on the Pentagon in which there were 683 arrests, but the significance of others was not apparent at the time. For example, no one outside Des Moines paid much attention when a group of high school pupils announced plans to wear black armbands in 1965 to show their opposition to the war. The school board quickly adopted a rule against armbands in school. Seven students defied the ban, were suspended, and went to court. In Tinker v. Des Moines Schools (393 U.S. 503, 1969), the Supreme Court held that a student's constitutional rights did not end at the schoolhouse door. The board had presented no evidence to show that wearing the armbands interfered in any way with classwork. Justice Black dissented vigorously on the grounds that school officials can set disciplinary standards and that schools are no place to exercise First Amendment claims!

A widespread form of protest was the burning of draft cards at public rallies. Congress responded in 1965 by making it a crime to "knowingly destroy" or "knowingly mutilate" a draft card, and almost before the ink was dry, federal prosecutors brought a number of actions. The trial courts differed, some finding it a symbolic act with First Amendment protection and some finding it unprotected.

David O'Brien, 19 years old, burned his draft card on the steps of the South Boston Courthouse before a crowd that included print and broadcast journalists. At his trial, he told the jury that he had burned his draft card publicly "so that other people would re-evaluate their positions with Selective Service, with the armed forces, and re-evaluate their place in the culture of today, to hopefully consider my position."

In 1968 the Supreme Court (United States v. O'Brien, 391 U.S. 367) found the law constitutional and in doing so rejected the symbolic speech argument. The court said that it had a duty to uphold any reasonable government regulation and said the burning ban had been enacted to make the Selective Service system work more smoothly, not primarily to punish protesters. Although there was an element of expression, it was outweighed by the government interest. Rather incredibly, the court said that the card itself, the wallet-sized piece of paper that would be replaced in days upon request if it were accidentally lost or destroyed, was a key element in the whole draft system.

Thomas Emerson (1970), Yale law professor, called the O'Brien decision "a serious setback for First Amendment theory." He chastized the court for not coming to grips with the central fact that the public burning was communication and therefore deserving of protection.

After the decision, protesters began mailing their cards back to boards rather than burning them. Although the draft card burners faced a maximum of five years and a $10,000 fine, a survey found that few judges handed out sentences of even half the maximum, and in many cases the sentences were suspended entirely.

Draft card burning was involved, indirectly, in the trial of Dr. Benjamin Spock, America's most famous pediatrician. The government accused him of conspiring with others to counsel draft-age men not to meet their military obligations. Most of the evidence centered on their organizing antiwar demonstrations in Washington, Boston, and New York in October 1967, at which hundreds of cards were burned.

In sentencing them to two years in prison, the judge could not resist a lecture:

> Every week in this court, young men are sentenced to three years in prison for evading the draft. It is reasonable to conclude that these defendants were instrumental in inciting some of these men to flout the law. Be they high or low, intellectuals as well as others must be deterred from violating the law. These defendants should not escape under the guise of free speech.

The Court of Appeals did not agree, although it avoided the First Amendment issues. It dismissed the convictions of Spock and one other for lack of evidence and remanded the other two for a new trial, a trial which the prosecutors chose not to pursue. The reversals drove another nail in the concept of conspiracy.

The most celebrated case was the 21-week trial of the "Chicago Seven," accused of inciting riots during the 1968 Democratic national convention. The federal jury found the defendants not guilty of conspiring to incite riots. (Two defendants were acquitted of all counts.) The convicted were David Dellinger and Rennie Davis (leaders of the National Mobilization Committee to End the War in Vietnam), and Jerry Rubin, Tom Hayden, and Abbie Hoffman, all prominent in the New Left antiwar movement. The judge sentenced them to five years each (plus fines). While the jury was out deliberating for five days, the judge imposed jail sentences on the defendants for contempt of court, ranging up to 2½ years. Then he turned to the flamboyant defense counsels and sentenced *them* to long jail terms for inciting the contempts during the trial.

The trial was bizarre, with the defendants sometimes bound and gagged to prevent outbursts. It was hard to tell who was more sarcastic, the defendants, the attorneys, or the judge; certainly the trial was no credit to any of them.

Three years later, the Court of Appeals reversed the convictions, holding that the "antagonistic" courtroom demeanor of the judge and prosecutors required reversal, even if other errors did not; however, the court refused to hold unconstitutional the 1968 antiriot act itself. In 1973 the contempt convictions were also reversed.

Many protests were staged at local draft boards. Although sometimes they involved destroying files, most were not violent. In 1965, two University of Michigan students who sat in at the Ann Arbor draft board lost their student deferments. Claiming that they were being punished for expressing their views, they asked the federal courts to issue injunctions to prevent reclassification. The Court of Appeals agreed, speaking through Harold R. Medina, the judge who presided in 1949 over the trial of the top Communists (see Chapter 4, this volume). Judge Medina wrote:

> The effect of the reclassification itself is immediately to curtail the exercise of First Amendment rights, for there can be no doubt that the threat of receiving a 1-A classification upon voicing dissent from our national policies has an immediate impact on the behavior.

By the time of Vietnam, most Americans received most of their news from television. Both doves and hawks wanted this powerful medium to present the war "realistically," meaning in a way that they found agreeable. Presidents Johnson and Nixon repeatedly claimed that TV news deliberately painted the war in a negative light, but a massive study by Braestrup (1977) detected no such ideological slant to what the networks showed. Others asked whether wars weren't always "negative."

There were attempts by both backers and critics of the war policy to use the Fairness Doctrine (see Chapter 7, this volume) to their own advantage. Unlike print media, broadcast media must have licenses. These periodic renewals provide opportunities for interest groups to pressure stations.

A conservative political group filed the most elaborate fairness claim in history with the Federal Communications Commission, charging that its monitoring of the CBS Evening News for 1972 and 1973 showed a distinctly antiwar tone. Its members counted and taped 274 segments in which either a CBS staffer or a person being interviewed discussed national security. It claimed that by a ratio of 2 to 1, they were against increased defense spending, building up the armed services, and so forth. The FCC rejected the fairness claim on the basis of the vague categories and definition of what constituted a "national security story." The Court of Appeals agreed with the commission about the methodological problems, but hinted that with a better focus and better methodology, such a broad fairness claim might someday be upheld.

Another Court of Appeals faced a fairness claim from doves, who insisted that if a station carried spot announcements urging enlistment in the armed forces, then it must carry counter-ads. The court turned down the claim, because the same station's news and public affairs programs had contained a significant amount of material that "presented the other side" of the war and military activities. That decision was made in 1977, long after the war.

When American and Vietnamese forces invaded Cambodia in the spring of 1970 to destroy the tactical and supply base of the communist forces, there were huge protests across the United States, the most tragic resulting in the shooting deaths of protesters at Kent State University.

After the massive air strikes at the end of 1971, the United States began pulling out its ground forces. Throughout the election year of 1972, bombings and withdrawals continued. Finally, a negotiated settlement at Paris allowed the United States to remove the last of its fighting forces in 1973. The next two unhappy years of warfare were left to the Vietnamese, and U.S. helicopters plucked the final Marine guards from the embassy in Saigon as the communists marched into the city. Congress made further military action in Southeast Asia illegal, just to formalize what public opinion had already concluded.

The longest war in American history involved 2.5 million American fighting men, most of whom were not sure why they were in Vietnam. Neither were their friends or families. There was no mobilization, and certainly few Americans felt that there was a real threat to their country.

There were unsuccessful attempts to get the courts to differentiate between declared and undeclared wars. The Supreme Court took the Massachusetts legislature's word for the fact it had passed a law asserting that no resident of that state had to serve outside the United States in order to set up a test case; the Court would not give what amounted to an "advisory opinion." Everyone recognized that limited wars were likely to be the pattern for the years ahead, so they worried about legal precedents.

At least two major principles emerge from the Vietnam protest cases: (1) Conspiracy is almost impossible to prove, and (2) General protests against war (or any other governmental) policy are protected, no matter how shrill. They are not insignificant principles. Certainly, they are a remarkable advance from 1917-18.

But there is another message from this quick review of the history of controls on dissent in American crises, and that is that many lessons have to be learned over again in each new crisis. Freedom is only as safe as public opinion will allow it to be.

# 4

## IDEOLOGUES WHO SHAPED
## THE FIRST AMENDMENT

**"Extremists" challenge a society's fundamental values and assumptions, and by doing so, they often force institutions to reevaluate those beliefs.**

In any society, most of the citizens are too busy "getting along" to concern themselves much with public policies or ideologies; however, there are some who believe so deeply in causes— religious, political, economic, or whatever—that they seek out controversy, and in doing so, they challenge community values. Often they are True Believers, courting martyrdom, daring society to try to crush them. The self-restraint that a society displays toward them is a measure of its own maturity. The obvious fact that these ideologues convert few others does not in any way negate their importance.

In this chapter, we consider three classes of challengers: pacifists, both traditional and not-so-traditional; ideologues of the left; and ideologues of the right.

### *PACIFISTS*

As we saw in the last chapter, in times of war a state expects its citizens to take up arms against its enemies. There have always been some who have refused to do this. In the United States, most such objectors have come from the traditional antiwar religious sects.

Any religious group that defies majority views or moral standards has faced persecution. Catholics and Jews were deprived of some rights and opportunities from the earliest American settlements, but they did not become major targets until they arrived in large numbers during the nineteenth century. Both aroused antagonisms, in part because their rituals and dogmas were "foreign" and, in the case of Catholics, because they operated their own schools. The Latter Day Saints, or Mormons, were hounded out of the East and then out of the Midwest before founding their own colony in Utah. The Mormons not only practiced polygamy, but they spoke out against other religions.

Religious questions are awkward for the legal system, for as Roche (1963) wrote, "the Court has to confront the perplexing problem of determining what society may or may not do with the disruptive messengers of God." Such persons are not likely to be pragmatists or compromisers, and assertions of faith are not subject to adjudication or ordinary processes of evidence. No issue has raised more such problems than compulsory service in the military. Quakers, Mennonites, the Amish, and Church of the Brethren have long histories of refusing to serve, and the Jehovah's Witnesses are a newer but at least equally adamant group. The last will be discussed separately.

The problem of who to excuse is an old and thorny one. James Madison tried, without success, to insert into the Bill of Rights a guaranteed exemption from military duty for those with such convictions. Large numbers obviously would rather not expose themselves to the hardships and dangers of war; the difficulty is in locating those who *cannot*. During the Civil War draft, some objectors hired substitutes, a perfectly acceptable and legal alternative, while others asked for and were usually granted exemptions.

The 1917 act permitted exemptions from combat—but not from noncombat—for members of religious groups with long traditions of opposing war. Of the 3 million men drafted in World War I, only 65,000 made the requests, most of which were granted. Of these, about 20,000 were inducted, four-fifths of whom agreed to alternate service. A hard core of about 200 refused to cooperate, even to register, and most of them went to prison. Socialist leader Norman Thomas (1923) was one. He later published a classic account of the entire issue in American history.

Many of the C.O.s were still in prison in 1928, when Rozika Schwimmer, a Hungarian pacifist and feminist, applied for American citizenship but was turned down because she refused to promise to take up arms for her new land. Although her being called to service was unlikely, the Supreme Court upheld the requirement (United States v. Schwimmer, 279 U.S. 644, 1929). Two years later, the court likewise upheld the government's refusal to grant citizenship to a Canadian theology professor who would swear to take up arms only in a war he deemed morally justifiable. (He was three decades ahead of his time with that argument.) It was

1946 before the court upheld the right of an alien to claim both pacifism and citizenship. In that case, a Canadian who was a Seventh-Day Adventist had declared himself willing to perform noncombatant service.

No one is sure how many conscientious objectors there were in World War II, because the Selective Service did not keep central records on how many entered with an agreement to serve in noncombatant roles. The official estimate is 25,000, but others suggest that there were four times that many; in any case, they constituted an infinitesimal percentage of the 13 million Americans who served between 1941 and 1945. The law provided "religious training and belief" rather than membership in a recognized peace church as the test for exemption. In Civilian Public Service camps, objectors could farm and do related labor. Many volunteered to be guinea pigs in medical experiments, and some 2,000 worked in mental hospitals.

In 1944, the Florida Supreme Court upheld the dismissal of a junior high school teacher because, with his C.O. status, he could not inculcate principles of "honesty and patriotism." The Illinois high court sustained the bar association's refusal to admit a pacifist to membership, and the Supreme Court of the United States upheld the decision.

A large share of the World War II total objectors were Jehovah's Witnesses. Their special problems are considered below.

What Trueblood (1966) said of the Quakers also applies to members of other traditional antiwar sects: World War II, with its genocide and concentration camps, presented new challenges to the conscience. The issue had always been stated in terms of what the individual should do when he became the personal object of attack or aggression, rather than in terms of his duty when the victim was a third party. Trueblood wrote: "The really difficult question before Quakers through the generations has not been, primarily, what a person ought to do if someone smites him on the cheek, but rather what he ought to do if someone is held in bondage who might be released or whose life might be saved, through the action of the person who is not personally threatened, but who knows that he is his brother's keeper." The pacifist also knew that if he did not participate, it meant that someone else would have to serve in his place.

During the 1960s, courts had to deal with two classes of objectors that they had avoided before: the nonreligious but secular objector, and the selective objector. The former insisted that they had moral tenets to prevent their participation, but no ties to traditional churches and no belief in a supreme being; the latter said that they opposed unjust wars, but not necessarily all wars.

Some courts had bought the religious-but-nonchurch type objection even during World War II, but it was 1965 before the Supreme Court allowed exemption for one whose personal code did not include belief in a supreme being.

Clearly, limited wars were the pattern for the future, and limited wars do not stir the near-universal support that is usually generated by all-out wars, with their attendant mobilization and strident patriotism. Limited wars are hard to sell at home, and there will be more formal objectors to serving in them. During the 1960s, at least, the courts refused to allow for selective objection, fearing it would open the way for massive claims.

## THE JEHOVAH'S WITNESSES

The Jehovah's Witnesses emerged in the 1870s. They believed that God's whole plan for mankind is revealed in the Bible—not only an explanation of all human history but a certain prediction of the future. Only members of the sect will be spared from the imminent violent end of the world (Armageddon). Members cannot swear that they are opposed to all wars, since they consider themselves soldiers in the "final war" with Satan. It is their duty to present an alternative to every human being on earth; hence their ardor in proselytizing. They assail all other religions as false, and they welcome verbal abuse and arrests as divine tests of their own faith.

Many of their leaders were arrested for "antiwar" activities during World War I, but it was during World War II that they became a major issue. By then, they had a skilled legal department, ready to appeal every conviction. Like St. Paul in the Roman Empire, the Witnesses have been experts in using the courts to further their cause, and in doing so, they have won many important civil liberties victories for the whole of society (Cole, 1955; Kim, 1964).

The ACLU's files bulge with complaints, not only about mistreatment of individual Witnesses, but of attacks by rock-throwing, club-wielding mobs upon conventions. In some cases, there were charges of collusion by local police in the attacks. The courtroom victories arose, not from these attacks, but from attempts to curb their distribution of literature and to make their children salute the American flag.

Door-to-door canvassing had been a primary tactic since the late 1920s, and local police often charged Witnesses with breaking Sunday blue laws, disturbing the peace, or distributing without a license. From the mid-1930s on, the society's legal department told those arrested not to pay a fine and, if necessary, to go to jail. Every adverse decision by a court was appealed, but these appeals, based strictly on the freedom of religion clause of the First Amendment, got nowhere. The Witnesses switched strategy and invoked freedom of expression in the 1938 landmark case of Lovell v. Griffin (303 U.S. 444).

Alma Lovell, a Witness, was convicted in the municipal court in Griffin, Georgia, and sentenced to 50 days in jail when she refused to pay her $50 fine. Like other members of her sect, she refused even to apply for a permit to pass out tracts. The Supreme Court reversed and applied liberty of the press to leaflets as well as to newspapers and periodicals. More importantly, the court insisted that the right to distribute was vital and inseparable from the right to publish. That was in 1938, and during the next term, the court overturned four more cities' ordinances limiting pamphlet distribution, either on time and place grounds or to prevent littering (Green, 1942).

In 1942 the Witnesses lost a distribution case in the Supreme Court by a 5-4 margin. An Alabama city had a $10 annual license fee for anyone engaging in business as a "book agent." The Witnesses, of course, refused to pay the fee and were arrested for distributing literature without the license. The court majority found nothing wrong with a fee that was collected from everyone seeking to distribute periodicals, books, or tracts. One year later, the court reversed itself and struck down such ordinances because, even though nondiscriminatory, they limited the flow of ideas.

In 1942 the Supreme Court unanimously upheld the conviction of a Jehovah's Witness for uttering "fighting words" to a policeman. He had called the officer a "God damned racketeer" and a "damned fascist," and these epithets led to a fist fight. In Chaplinsky v. New Hampshire (315 U.S. 568), the court reasoned:

There are certain well-defined and narrowly limited classes of speech, the prevention and punishment of which have never been thought to raise any Constitutional problem. These include the lewd and obscene, the profane, the libelous, and the insulting or "fighting" words—those which by their very utterance inflict injury or tend to incite an immediate breach of the peace. It has been well observed that such utterances are no essential part of any exposition of ideas, and are of such slight social value as a step to truth that any benefit that may be derived from them is clearly outweighed by the social interest in order and morality.

The group's most dramatic Supreme Court victory was on the question of compulsory flag salutes in the public schools. About half the states had such laws, and as late as 1940 their constitutionality had been upheld by the Supreme Court. Witness attorneys continued to test them, and in 1943, in the middle of the biggest war in American history, the court reversed itself (West Virginia v. Barnett, 319 U.S. 105). The justices said that while furthering the feeling of national unity was a legitimate goal, it was not one that could be coerced through laws. The constitutional interests of those who had conscientious problems with participating in the ceremony were greater (Manwaring, 1962).

They are a tenacious, as well as a litigious lot. Cole estimates that between 1935 and 1950 some 10,000 Witnesses were arrested, usually in direct attempts to test the constitutionality of certain ordinances or laws. They won about half the trials but 150 of 190 appeals, including about 40 at the Supreme Court level. Through their litigation, more than 25 different types of legal restrictions were erased in the United States. They also challenged similar laws in at least 20 other nations. Hitler jailed more than 10,000 Jehovah's Witnesses.

## IDEOLOGUES OF THE LEFT

Daniel Boorstin (1953) called the absence of ideology "the genius of American politics." Certainly, labor unions and political parties based on ideology have fared less well in the United States than in most other parts of the world.

The Communist Party, even more than the various branches of socialism, was rooted in the aliens and immigrants from Europe and had little success in converting many native-born Americans. In the public mind, "bomb throwing" was almost an automatic modifier for "Bolshevik." They were all seen as radicals with "un-American" ideas.

There were "red scares" following both world wars. The Justice Department swept down on aliens suspected of furthering the communist cause in 1919 and early 1920, and actually deported many "undesirable aliens." Feelings ran high against Bolshevism, even in the smallest inland towns. Mobs augmented the official crackdown; however, the spasm ended as quickly as it began, and the anti-alienism was channeled into restrictive immigration laws in 1921 and 1924. These virtually cut off the flow of immigration from Eastern and Southern Europe, the places from which most of those deemed "troublemakers" had come (see Chapter 6, this volume).

It is worth remembering that leftists were the principals in the series of important cases emerging out of World War I. Schenck, Abrams, and Gitlow all went to jail (see Chapter 3), but the Supreme Court expanded the rights of all Americans in the process of upholding the convictions. A streetcar conductor won a major Supreme Court victory for free expression in 1937. Dirk DeJonge was convicted under Oregon law for presiding over a public meeting, called by the Communist Party, to protest the brutality of Portland police in handling a longshoremen's strike. Although the meeting was orderly, DeJonge had urged those present to go out and recruit more members for the Communist Party. The Oregon courts said that met their test of incitement to criminal action, but the Supreme Court disagreed. In DeJonge v. Oregon (299 U.S. 353), the unanimous court ruled:

> The greater the importance of safeguarding the community from incitements to the overthrow of our institutions by force and violence, the more imperative is the need to preserve inviolate the constitutional rights of free speech, free press and free assembly in order to maintain the opportunity for free political discussion, to the end that government may be responsible to the will of the people and that changes, if desired, may be obtained by peaceful means. Therein lies the security of the Republic, the very foundation of constitutional government.

The decision underlined the principle that expression not linked to the use of force and violence was clearly protected by the First and Fourteenth Amendments. Within a few years, the Supreme Court also found unconstitutional a part of a state law against displaying a red flag (the symbol of communism) and reversed the conviction of another communist under a state insurrection law.

Lens (1964) considered the post-World War II anti-communist crusade insidious precisely because it was more sophisticated than its predecessors:

> The number of people who have been jailed for communist views has been small; the number who have lost jobs because of blacklisting practices is no more than a few thousand. America had no concentration camps and its FBI is far from a Gestapo, as some leftists have insisted. So many basic traditions are being eroded, however, that the groundwork is laid for far more serious repressions. . . . Pressures to conform have become so great that many dissenters limit their criticism. By a subtle process, the individualistic elan has been subverted to a considerable extent by mass conformity. It is beside the point to say that many of these things happened before. They have never happened for so long a period, and with so little opposition.

It is not quite accurate to call the Alien Registration Act of 1940 a wartime measure. It was enacted in June 1940, more than a year before the United States declared war, but it was the product of alien fears. More than 40 laws to restrict aliens were introduced into the 1939-40 session of Congress, and these were consolidated into one section of the omnibus Alien Registration Act. That section was commonly called the Smith Act after the Virginia congressman who introduced it.

The Smith Act prohibited three kinds of activities: (1) advocating forceful overthrow of the government; (2) organizing a group for such advocacy; and (3) belonging to a group engaging in such advocacy. While its reach was similar to that of the Espionage Act, this one did not need a formal declaration of war to go into effect. Maximum punishment was 20 years plus a fine, and for good measure, it provided that one convicted under the act was not eligible for federal employment for at least five years. (It is hard to imagine that a person convicted under the law would be a top candidate for a government post anyway.)

Attorney General Francis Biddle authorized the first trial under the Smith Act of some Trotskyites in St. Paul in 1940. In his autobiography, he said he permitted the trial because he thought the Smith Act unconstitutional and that the courts would agree. He was surprised and disappointed when the Supreme Court upheld the convictions and the law.

In all, 29 members of the splinter leftist group were arrested after raids on their headquarters. Indicted under both the Smith Act and the 1861 Treason Act, 17 defendants were convicted under the former and exonerated under the latter. The decision in the five-week trial came in just in time for the Trotskyites to face sentencing on the Monday morning that the United States declared war on Japan, 8 December 1941. Considering the timing, it is surprising that the sentences ranged only from 12 to 16 months.

In 1949 the government brought to trial the twelve top leaders of the American Communist Party, including its chairman, Eugene Dennis. They were accused of reconstituting the party in 1945 and of conspiring to advocate violent overthrow of the government. For nine months, the government sought to show that these men had done more than discuss doctrines; rather, they had advocated illegal violence. Thousands of pages from tracts, newspapers, and books were read into the record. Judge Medina instructed the jury carefully; in order to convict, they must find advocacy, and they did. In 1951 the Supreme Court upheld the convictions in Dennis v. United States (341 U.S. 494). In Chief Justice Vinson's plurality opinion, he wrote that it was not unreasonable that "the societal value of speech must, on occasion, be subordinated to other values and considerations." He used the clear-and-present-danger test, first used by Holmes 32 years earlier, in deciding that the gravity of the danger posed by Dennis and his cohorts was sufficient to convict. The Smith Act was constitutional.

Federal prosecuters immediately started gathering information to prosecute the next lower echelon of communists. Many actions began, but they came to a screeching halt with the court's 1957 decision in Yates v. United States (354 U.S. 298). In that trial of 14 communist leaders, the judge had not insisted that the jury distinguish between advocacy of abstract doctrines and advocacy aimed at promoting unlawful action. The Supreme Court found that a fatal flaw and reversed the convictions. With that, defendants in many pending cases were dismissed, and the Smith Act lapsed into disuse. It was finally repealed in 1978.

There were fifteen trials under the Smith Act with about 100 defendants. Pember (1969) found that in none did the government even attempt to show that any of the writings, speeches, or meetings ever converted or affected anyone; certainly, the American Communist Party was not a rousing popular success.

Another fruit of the postwar anticommunist hysteria was a spate of cases involving contempt of Congress, often because a witness refused to tell investigating committees about his past associations. These committees investigated all sorts of institutions, including the movie industry, the broadcast networks, and major newspapers, searching for alleged "communists" or "communist sympathizers." The contempt often arose when the witness refused to name those he had known or seen at left-wing rallies or meetings many years before. Balky witnesses found the courts more sympathetic to Fifth Amendment (self-incrimination) claims than to First Amendment (expression rights) claims. The courts also refused to find a First Amendment right to travel to restricted nations (such as Cuba) to gather information.

## IDEOLOGUES OF THE RIGHT

While there have always been spokesmen for ultraconservatism, they have seldom coalesced into political parties in the United States. Notable exceptions were the Know-Nothings and Anti-Masons of the nineteenth century. Those who have espoused such ideas in the twentieth century ususally have done so, not under a political party banner, but under the guise of nationalism or moralism.

Real right-wing groups—as opposed to those representing conservative, often probusiness, views—have been recruited largely from the lower socioeconomic strata. Many activists, frustrated in their personal lives, act out their moral indignation born in resentment. Lipset (1959) found among the working classes of all nations the heaviest racial prejudice, the most readiness to turn to violence as a solution for social problems, and the most avid nationalism.

Perhaps the major civil liberty development of this century was the growth of civil liberty elites, groups willing to fight for the legal rights of those whose ideas they often found abhorrent. Most notable were the Anti-Defamation League and the American Civil Liberties Union.

Most of these defendants have been associated with some font or other of the Ku Klux Klan or the American Nazi Party. Although the KKK has been the target of restrictive legislation for more than a century (such as laws requiring publication of their membership lists or prohibiting masks in public demonstration), their cases have left relatively little impression on American jurisprudence. Certainly, it has been far less than that left by the Nazis and their imitators.

No laws have ever been effective in curbing hatemongers. Not only do they thrive on persecution but they take advantange of the attendant publicity to present their message to an enlarged audience. Illinois, for example, used a criminal libel statute to prosecute the president of a rag-tag group calling itself "The White Circle League." The law prohibited publications portraying "depravity, criminality, unchastity, or lack of virtue of a class of citizens of any race, color, creed, or religion" that subjected those described to "contempt, derision, or obloquy or which is productive of breach of the peace or riots."

The leader was arrested handing out leaflets calling on Chicago officials to halt the "further encroachment, harassment and invasion of white people, their property, neighborhoods and persons, by the Negro." It called on white people to unite against "becoming mongrelized."

Hateful as those ideas might be to many, like almost any issued by such demagogues, they focus on issues of great interest in the community, issues that need to be addressed even today. Whether their proponents will be prosecuted depends largely on the attitudes of the current occupant of the prosecutor's office.

Although the court upheld the law (Beauharnais v. Illinois, 343 U.S. 250 1952), Illinois soon repealed it. Constitutional lawyers consider criminal libel an ineffective and dangerous way to try to limit demagogues.

It was an article in the journal of the John Birch Society that led to the major restatement of the law of public libel in 1974 in Gertz v. Welch (418 U.S. 323). The society was essentially the creation of Robert Welch, an ultraconservative candy millionaire. The magazine was devoted largely to exposing the "communist menace," and by naming a prominent Chicago attorney as one of those engaged in a campaign to undermine faith in the police of the nation, it laid the groundwork for the suit.

For the decade preceding his assassination in 1967, George Lincoln Rockwell, the head of the American Nazi Party, spent much of his time embarrassing municipal officials by requesting permits to speak in public parks. When they refused, and he went to court, he received the publicity he sought. No estimate ever placed Rockwell's membership at more than 500. Rockwell knew there was a long series of court decisions (won by religious, civil rights, and labor organizations) that made it clear that while cities could require such permits, they had to issue them pretty much on a first-come, first-served basis.

In one of these incidents, Rockwell had been refused a license to speak in Union Square in New York City. The first court declared that the denial was reasonable because the Constitution did not require city officials "to loose self-confessed advocates of violence upon a community at a time and place where it is inevitable that public disorder and riot will occur."

The higher state court, however, reversed this in 1961, on the ground that the issuing officer had no business guessing about what the speech might contain or what reactions it might evoke. The court could find no evidence that the speech would have provoked immediate and irreparable damage; certainly, it was unlikely to convince any significant number of listeners to commit illegal acts. The court outlined important principles in the opinion, including the following:

> The unpopularity of views, their shocking quality, their obnoxious- ness, and even their alarming impact is not enough. Otherwise, the preacher of any strange doctrine could be stopped: the anti-racist himself could be suppressed, if he undertakes to speak in "restricted" areas; and one who asks that public schools be open indiscriminately to all ethnic groups could be lawfully suppressed, if only he chose to speak where persuasion is needed most.

> Only if Rockwell speaks criminally . . . can his right to speak be cut off. If he does not speak criminally, then, of course, his right to speak may not be cut off, no matter how offensive his speech may be to others. Instead, his right, and that of those who wish to listen to him, must be protected, no matter how unpleasant the assignment.

> In summary, the key to understanding is really very simple: The right of free expression is not to be entrusted to administrative previous restraint for contemplated violation of law, but such expression is not immune from punishment after the fact for what has been said, by judicial process. This is not unreasonable. History everywhere has shown the executive sometimes to establish tyranny and dictatorship by the powers of suppression.

> Surely, there is risk in denying prior restraint. It is a price paid for liberty while order is to be preserved by the sanction of punishment after the fact. It is the price paid for not having the policeman or the Commissioner as censor, while leaving the courts, disciplined by appellate review and the rules of evidence, to provide punishment under criminal standards for the unlawful act already committed. But the risk is not so great as to be intolerable in a civilized, law-abiding community.

Rockwell won several other such decisions, and sometimes he did not even take the trouble to make the speech once he had won.

More than a few of these legal actions were carried out by the American Civil Liberties Union. On at least one occasion, Rockwell turned to the Jewish attorney from the ACLU who had just won a case for him and told him he need not think his actions would spare him from the gas chambers!

The Nazis are a symbol of everything most Americans find abhorrent; therefore, they serve as a litmus test for the real level of freedom in the society. After all, it is the way the majority treats those it hates that really defines this freedom. If the Nazis had not existed, we would have had to invent them.

But they do exist, and in 1977 they gained center stage with their efforts to demonstrate in predominantly Jewish Skokie, Illinois. The ACLU's defense of their right to march lost the civil rights organization thousands of members and put it in serious financial jeopardy.

The fact situation is complex, and the flurry of legal battles can be passed over here. Briefly, Chicago had raised to $250,000 the price a damage insurance bond to demonstrate in a park in a neighborhood where racial tensions were inflamed. While that was being appealed, the head of the local Nazi splinter group, called the National Socialist Party of America, wrote to a dozen suburban communities to request permits to demonstrate there. While the others ignored the letter, Skokie reacted by raising its fee to $350,000. That, too, was appealed. The fight over the park permit had not created much publicity, but this was different. Skokie included in its population nearly 7,000 survivors of Nazi death camps or their relatives (Hamlin, 1980).

While it is understandable that these residents did not want to see swastikas and other reminders of the Holocaust, it was precisely that hatred of symbols that the Nazis manipulated. Frank Collin, the leader of the NSPA, had no more than two dozen members, and according to Hamlin (1980), "The dread brutal Fascists Collin leads are in fact young street kids who are rarely brutal and hardly dreadful, and whose arrest records run to disorderly conduct born of an occasional street scuffle." They created their illusion by misdirecting the attention of their critics from pitiful realities to the powerful symbols of Nazism.

The executive director of the ACLU during the crisis, Aryeh Neier (1979), said that while most newspapers supported with editorials the right of the Nazis to demonstrate, the letters to the editor in the same papers ran heavily against that position. Neier, who not only was Jewish but had been born in Berlin and as a youth had to flee Hitler, was stunned by the vehemence.

The welter of cases, appeals, and reversals that grew out of the Skokie matter really centered on two legal principles, the "heckler's veto" and the "fighting words" doctrine.

Under the former, the argument is that the speech must be blocked because it will be offensive to those who might hear it and therefore might provoke hecklers to violence. That logic certainly would have barred civil rights marches in the South in the 1960s, because those marches could and often did provoke precisely those reactions. To silence the speaker because he might upset some of those in the audience is to bar all unpopular speech.

The Illinois Supreme Court disposed of the "fighting words" argument when it lifted the injunction against displaying the swastika in the planned parade. Hateful reminders though they might be, they were symbolic speech and therefore protected. The "fighting words" doctrine was a narrow one, developed to exempt epithets hurled at an unsuspecting listener, and certainly not to be extended to a well-advertised and scheduled demonstration. Anyone who did not want to see swastikas could stay home, the court said.

But there never was a march in Skokie, in spite of the court's upholding the right of the Nazis to demonstrate there. Collin was afraid that the police might not be able to control the counterdemonstrators, and so he agreed to use the plaza at the Federal Building in downtown Chicago instead. The police escorted his little coterie of brownshirted followers in and out of the plaza, but the thousands who assembled made so much noise that no one could hear what Collin said over his bullhorn during the fifteen minutes he was there. This was in June 1978. The next month, the NASL demonstrated in the Chicago park they had requested fourteen months earlier, and again the counterdemonstrators drowned them out.

Collin disappeared from the news until early 1980, when he was arrested, convicted, and sentenced to seven years in prison for indecent liberties with under-age boys.

# EDITORS WHO SHAPED
# THE FIRST AMENDMENT

**Antiestablishment papers and magazines test the limits of community toleration and, therefore, of free expression. The "regular" press is not always at their side in the ensuing legal battles.**

This is the story of three editors whose defiant actions helped define free expression for everyone. All three edited small publications that were considered less than respectable by many. Except for the fact that all three operated in the Upper Midwest, they had little in common. One published a scandal sheet in the Twin Cities in the 1920s, another a youth-oriented underground paper in the 1970s, and the third a monthly magazine that was perennially on the financial ropes.

It is less a story of what they did or wrote than it is of the attempts by the government to prosecute them. Such editors have less political clout than, say, the New York *Times* or *Time* magazine, and are therefore more inviting targets. They are less martyred than the Abolitionist editor lynched by an Illinois mob before the Civil War, the Ohio newspaper editor gunned down in the 1920s by mobsters, or the Arizona reporter whose car was blown up by underworld figures in the 1970s. But the three we have selected left a legal heritage.

We are not examining here the special kind of heroism shown by media executives who, knowing it will cost them untold legal fees and hassles, encourage staff members to defy attempts to keep them from publishing legitimate news. Some of these challenges, such as those to judicial gag orders, are discussed in other chapters.

Our three editors were hell-raisers. They set out to stir the public conscience, but they were not quite the "ideologues" discussed in the last chapter. These three were journalists with more than a touch of Tom Paine in them. The Founding Fathers wanted to protect the Tom Paines.

## JAY NEAR AND HIS SCANDAL SHEET

As we saw, the men who wrote the Constitution and added the first ten amendments agreed that freedom of the press meant freedom from prior restraints. They argued about how much more it might mean, but they did not argue about that. It seems ironic, therefore, that the Supreme Court should have to face that question in 1931. As is always true in a legal case, there were other issues involved, and the other issues threatened to strangle the fundamental one of prior restraint.

During the late nineteenth and early twentieth centuries, the Supreme Court consistently interpreted the Fourteenth Amendment as protecting property but not individual rights. It would sanction a state's use of police or militia to put down strikes or other disturbances so long as it could be claimed the actions were taken to protect safety, health, or morals. Most local judges willingly granted injunctions to halt picketing or boycotts and jailed those who violated the orders. If all else failed, police could always use the local "catch-all" ordinances against vagrancy, trespassing, or disturbing the peace against "troublemakers."

The Supreme Court seldom reviewed state prosecutions for obscenity, blasphemy, libel, or contempt by publication, and when it did it seemed more concerned with asserting that there were definite limits to free expression than in expanding those limits. So long as one stuck to the literal wording of the First Amendment ("Congress shall make no law. . ."), it was possible to argue the First Amendment was almost absolute. The federal government was not repressing expression; the state and local governments were. But the Supreme Court refused to rein them in.

As we saw in Chapter 3, the federal as well as the state governments enacted laws that punished unpopular expression in World War I. In the early 1920s the Supreme Court reviewed a series of convictions under these federal acts and thus had to come to grips with some basic issues of free expression. In 1925 it took the momentous step of reviewing Benjamin Gitlow's conviction under a *state* sedition statute.

Throughout the nation during the 1920s, there were demands to clean up the newsstands. Some were offended by the new tabloid newspapers, with their emphasis on sex, crime, and scandal; others wanted to ban the new confession magazines; still others were disgusted by local sheets that "told all" about prominent citizens. Minnesota enacted the control that drew the most attention and ultimately provided a historic victory for free expression in the Supreme Court.

The law, which drew much praise at the time of its passage in 1925, was admirable in its simplicity. A county attorney could request that a district judge issue a temporary restraining order against an obscene or "malicious, scandalous, and defamatory" publication. The accused publisher would then have to appear in court and try to convince the judge that his publication was not a public nuisance. If he failed, the judge would make the publication ban permanent. It was essentially the same procedure long used to halt those who poured sewage into rivers or whose plants created odors that annoyed neighbors.

It was a cheap, fast, and efficient solution. Its backers insisted it was not classic, prepublication censorship because the orders were issued only after a publisher had demonstrated his obnoxious nature. Responsible publishers had nothing to fear, its backers assured everyone, and most Minnesota editors agreed.

The law was introduced by a legislator from the Duluth area, who made no secret of the fact that he wanted to "get" the Duluth *Rip-Saw*. The editor of the little weekly had published articles for years accusing public officials of ties to gambling and vice operations. At least some of them were true, as Friendly (1981) has documented. The editor was publishing material that no other newspaper would touch. He was the first to be enjoined under the new law, but he died before the ban could be made permanent. (In this there is a curious historical parallel with Benjamin Franklin Bache. Bache, the main target of the Sedition Act of 1978 and the first to be indicted under it, died before he could be convicted.) The little Duluth weekly expired with its editor, the legal issue unresolved.

Other Minnesota politicians had their own candidates for "public nuisances." One was the *Saturday Press* in the Twin Cities. Although this paper wasn't started until 1927, its owners were old hands at editing on the fringes of respectability. Howard Guilford had published a series of small scandal sheets since 1913. His specialty was exposing the sexual peccadillos of prominent people in Minneapolis and St. Paul; many suggested his real specialty was collecting fees from rich people whose exposes he did *not* publish. Jay M. Near had worked with him, off and on, since 1916. Near's blasts were virulently anti-Semitic, anti-Catholic, anti-black, and anti-labor. Since the Twin Cities were notorious for corruption and for the way the police (and the daily newspapers) looked the other way, Guilford and Near found plenty of targets for their purple prose. Many of the officials they accused of underworld ties were a few years later convicted of those very charges.

Their newest joint venture, the *Saturday Press*, had hardly hit the streets before it was enjoined under the nuisance law. The order was made permanent in late 1927 with hardly a whisper of protest from the establishment newspapers. In this, the Minnesota newspapers were not unique. With notable exceptions, most of the press has never supported those who challenge political or social orthodoxy. Lofton (1981) concluded that the American press was seldom sensitive to civil liberties issues. On ideological issues, such as labor radicalism, socialism, and communism, he found "leading newspapers have spoken almost with one voice in denying the applicability of the First Amendment." Nor did they support publications accused of obscenity or, like the *Saturday Press,* that challenged community standards. Other scholars have given general newspapers better marks for protecting freedoms. Bowles (1977) studied the editorial reactions of sixteen major American newspapers to civil liberty issues in 1920 and 1940, dates chosen for more than their symmetry. These were years in which Congress was debating sedition bills and courts were deciding important civil liberty cases. In both years, the editorials were predominantly in favor of the civil liberty position.

The real hero of the Near case was Robert McCormick, publisher of the Chicago *Tribune.* McCormick's paper was the bastion of conservatism, for decades the target of liberal and even moderate wrath. McCormick himself was a tireless champion of the First Amendment, and he recognized in Near's plight a threat to all the press. Near wrote to McCormick, as he wrote to just about anyone he could think of, for financial assistance. Unlike most of the others, the millionaire publisher from Chicago responded. Friendly (1981) examined the internal memos between the publisher and his attorney and concluded that it was the attorney's enthusiasm that finally convinced McCormick to lend the financial assistance and the prestige of his paper to defending Near. In one of these memos, the attorney warned McCormick:

> If this decision stands, any newspaper in Minnesota which starts a crusade against gambling, vice or other evils, may be closed down . . .

without a trial by jury. . . . How easy it would be for a "small" administration, through control of the legislature, to pass a like statute in Illinois or some other state.

McCormick turned the case over to his own legal firm, and in spite of complaints by Near himself (Guilford had by then stepped out and was not involved in the appeal), the *Tribune* lawyers handled the case all the way to the Supreme Court. Eventually, McCormick bullied the American Newspaper Publishers Association into supporting the appeal with a resolution and with a token financial grant, but many publishers remained convinced that it was the wrong case at the wrong time. Their successors would take the same view about the *Progressive* case a half-century later.

One day in March 1930, both Chief Justice William Howard Taft and Associate Justice Edward T. Sanford died. They were replaced before the Near case was heard by Charles Evans Hughes and Owen J. Roberts, both of whom were in the 5-to-4 majority for Near. Hughes, in fact, wrote the opinion.

In the oral argument, the attorney for Minnesota insisted that there was no prior restraint involved since the injunction was issued only after the *Saturday Press* showed itself a nuisance by defaming public officials. He said that the law helped "purify" the press and control blackmailers. He was interrupted by Associate Justice Louis D. Brandeis, the only Jew on the court, who now challenged the state's case against the paper which so often had attacked Jews. The newspaper had exposed corruption, and surely that was in the public interest. He went on:

> Of course there was defamation; you cannot disclose evil without naming the doers of evil. It is difficult to see how one can have a free press and the protection it affords in the democratic community without the privilege this act seems to limit. You are dealing here not with a sort of scandal too often appearing in the press, and which ought not to appear in the interest of anyone, but with a matter of prime interest to every American citizen. What sort of matter could be more privileged?

Brandeis then wanted to know how such a campaign could be effective if it were not continued. In short, he rejected the idea of halting a publication for what it had published or for what it might publish in the future. The attorney turned to the 89-year-old Oliver Wendell Holmes and reminded him that 24 years earlier he had written an opinion permitting the punishment of newspapers for what they had published. Holmes smiled and said, "I was much younger when I wrote that opinion than I am now, Mr. Markham. If I did make such a holding, I now have a different view."

At the very time of the hearing, the Minnesota legislature was moving to repeal the law under which Near had been convicted more than three years earlier. McCormick did not want the case mooted, and neither did Near. The Minnesota House voted for repeal, but the Senate did not go along.

The Supreme Court handed down its decision in Near v. Minnesota (283 U.S. 697) on 1 June 1931, the final day of the term. Hughes anchored his opinion in Blackstonian quotations against prior restraints, and in Madisonian arguments against inhibiting the press in its role as critic of government. The key paragraph read:

> If we cut through mere details of procedure, the operation and effect of the statute in substance is that public authorities may bring the owner or publisher of a newspaper or periodical before a judge upon a charge of conducting a business of publishing scandalous and defamatory matter—in particular that the matter consists of charges against public officers or official dereliction—and unless the owner or publisher is able and disposed to bring competent evidence to satisfy the judge that the charges are true and are published with good motives and for justifiable ends, his newspaper or periodical is suppressed and further publication is made punishable by contempt. This is the essence of censorship.

Hughes's opinion conceded that there might be rare situations to justify prior restraints, and he cited as examples information about the sailing of troop ships in wartime or certain obscene materials. He found no such justification in the case of Minnesota's action against Jay Near. The court's dissent, incidentally, was written by Pierce Butler, a native of Minnesota.

Looking back during a symposium marking the fiftieth anniversary of the Near decision, historian Paul L. Murphy (1981) emphasized three strands in the decision. In the First Amendment area, the ruling was strongly "marketplace" in its tone. That is, it stressed the importance of the press as watchdog on government and worked its way around Near's motives, bigotry, and irresponsibility. In a different context, the ruling was a step away from the criminality that had been associated with certain forms of expression, belief, and association (as expressed in Prohibition), and which by the end of the 1920s was being seen as unwarranted interference with personal rights and choices. Finally, Murphy saw the Near case as an attempt to move the country away from the use of informal local controls to limit freedom of expression. It was one of the first times the Supreme Court had recognized the essence of such controls and was not fooled by the alleged procedural safeguards.

It is foolhardy to speculate on what might have happened if one of the five justices in the majority had voted to uphold the Minnesota law. Certainly, other states were contemplating such nuisance laws to control their feistier newspapers.

What of Jay Near himself? During the years of litigation, he served as propagandist and ghost writer for an unsuccessful candidate for governor who smeared his opponent as a tool of "Jew pigs," "thugs," and "communists." A few months after the Supreme Court victory, his Saturday Press reappeared, as prickly and combative as ever; however, within a few months he sold the paper to his old partner, Guilford. Unknown assassins gunned Guilford down in 1934 and Near died quietly in a Minneapolis hospital in 1936, almost unnoticed and unmourned. His short obituary in the Minneapolis papers did not even mention his Supreme Court case, although the one in the Chicago Tribune did.

## MARK KNOPS AND HIS UNDERGROUND PAPER

The youth-oriented underground papers that blossomed in the late 1960s and early 1970s offended many people; that was one of their goals. Stridently antiestablishment in character, they bristled with four-letter words and explicit artwork. Some of those whose noses were tweaked took reprisals. Merchants who might have been inclined to advertise were pressured not to. Many of the papers had great difficulty finding a printer, even when finances were not a problem (which they usually were).

Police raided offices on various pretexts, usually obscenity, and hauled off tons of material. Editors were prosecuted for violating seldom-enforced local ordinances, and street vendors who hawked the issues were bullied and sometimes arrested for littering or for failure to carry the proper permits. Many of the papers gloried in their martyrdom, and it is impossible to say how many succumbed

because of the harassment and how many because they tired of the
hard work of putting out the issues.

As Fred Graham (1972) has documented, the established media
or media organizations seldom came to the legal defense of the
underground editors. In that respect they fared worse than Jay Near
had 40 years earlier. There was a long string of legal hassles, mostly
by local police, who were frequently called "pigs" or worse in the
pages of the newspapers. Many governmental agencies refused to
issue staff members credentials or press passes. As Graham wrote:
"Underground publications are almost always out of favor with
local governments and in bad odor with other influential circles in
the communities where they are published. They have a greater
proclivity for antagonizing officials than the established press,
unaccompanied by prestige or self-protective power." That, of
course, was exactly their purpose and their societal value.

Editors of "regular" newspapers did not like to be associated with
the scruffy elements of their business and even avoided, whenever
they could, legal questions involving the college or high school
press. One case arose where they had no choice but to get involved.
In 1971 police moved into a Stanford University building to remove
demonstrators. During the ensuing melee, several policemen were
injured. The next day, the Stanford *Daily* published several
photographs of the confrontation. In an effort to find out which
students had attacked the officers, county law enforcement officials
obtained a warrant to search the campus newspaper's newsroom to
find more pictures and negatives. There was no allegation against
any member of the *Daily* staff. It was strictly a third-party search;
that is, it was to gather information that might be used in
prosecuting others. While such searches are not uncommon in
many areas of the law, attorneys argued that they were potentially
harmful for newspapers. Reporters would have to worry about
protecting the confidentiality of sources in notes they retained. The
threat of police swooping down would have a chilling effect on the
entire news operation, the attorneys who represented the press of
the nation argued. They appealed the action all the way to the
Supreme Court on First Amendment grounds; however, in Zurcher
v. Stanford Daily (436 U.S. 547, 1978), the court decided on Fourth
Amendment grounds. The justices found the raid justified, noting
that there was no special sanctity to a newsroom. The resulting howl
from editorial writers across the country prompted Congress to

enact a law that set stringent requirements on any police requests for a newsroom search warrant.

*Kaleidoscope,* however, was not published at a respected university. It was a genuine counterculture underground newspaper. Unlike many others of its kind, however, it appeared on a regular schedule. Its founder was a former Milwaukee *Journal* staff member who knew news, layout, and basic business principles. Glessing (1970) called it "one of the most carefully edited papers in the underground." The paper started with 3,500 copies and one edition, but by 1969 it had grown to 40,000 copies with editions in Milwaukee, Chicago, and Madison. The editors even published an insert for smaller underground papers in Minneapolis and Indianapolis.

Each issue carried a wide range of stories. Glessing cites a typical 1969 issue containing stories on police harassment, high school turmoil, criticism of American society in general, women's liberation, how to get and use drugs, plus underground comics and pictures of nudes. Like many of the 300 to 400 underground papers publishing regularly, *Kaleidoscope* mixed radical politics and radical culture, with many articles on rock music and survival information for its alienated readers.

In 1969, *Kaleidoscope* published this as part of its manifesto:

> American capitalism says graduate and leave; we want $10 million to build a community; American capitalism says tear down the Co-op for a Left Turn lane; we say tear down all the left turn lanes, all the used car lots.... In one night of frenzied dadaistic energy, plant trees, flowers, make Madison beautiful. . . . We want the feel of life in a young girl's sweatshirt and jeans, not the feel of death on the dashboard of an Olds. . . . We will throw off the yoke of oppression. We will have poets in our drugstores and supermarkets . . . and we will have workers control, students control, womens control, lovers control and childrens control. We need to found a Left which speaks to each corner of our existence, A MARXISM OF EVERYDAY LIFE.

The paper was soon to be faced with more immediate problems. Early on an August morning in 1970, a bomb ripped through a research building on the campus of the University of Wisconsin, killing one and injuring several others. Two days later, *Kaleidoscope* published a long story, headlined "The Bombers Tell Why and What Next," which justified the action as necessary to restructure society. It was, in fact, almost classical anarchist rhetoric.

A grand jury subpoenaed the editor, Mark Knops, who at 27 was older than most of his readers. While not a founder of *Kaleidoscope,* he had been through several legal hassles. On his attorney's advice, he first refused to answer any questions and then agreed to answer all but five that sought the identity of the persons who gave him the letter.

Knops was sentenced to six months in jail for contempt, and he appealed to the Wisconsin Supreme Court. The court rejected his contention that he needed to guarantee anonymity in order to publish the important information for his readers:

> In a disorderly society such as we are currently experiencing it may well be appropriate to curtail in a very minor way the free flow of information, if such curtailment will serve the purpose of restoring an atmosphere in which all of our fundamental freedoms can flourish. One exceedingly fundamental freedom which the public is currently doing without is the freedom to walk into public buildings without having to fear for one's life. If the public were faced with a choice between learning the identity of the bombers or reading their justifications for anarchy, it seems safe to assume that the public would choose to learn their identities.

One precedent cited by the Wisconsin Supreme Court in its rejection of Knops's First Amendment claim involved the editor of the student newspaper at the University of Oregon, who in 1969 refused to tell a grand jury the names of students she had seen smoking marijuana. Although the Oregon Supreme Court upheld her contempt conviction, her light fine and appeals costs were borne by media organizations, and she became something of a celebrity.

The court majority insisted that the fact that the bombers were still at large proved that Knops's testimony was essential; however, one justice noted that both state and federal officials had admitted that they knew the identities of the bombers and were already searching for them. (They soon found them and sent them to prison, all without Knops's evidence.)

On the surface, the decision was a defeat for free expression; however, almost in passing, the Wisconsin justices asserted flatly that an underground paper and its editor were entitled to the same protections as a "regular" paper and its editor. There had been hints of this in earlier decisions by other courts, but this was a bald assertion of equality. It did not keep Mark Knops out of jail, but then, Abrams, Schenck, Gitlow, and countless other figures in more famous cases had also gone to jail in cases later used to liberalize the interpretation of freedom.

## ERWIN KNOLL AND HIS MAGAZINE

Erwin Knoll is as different from Jay Near and Mark Knops as *The Progressive* is from the *Saturday Press* or *Kaleidoscope*. Knoll was a distinguished writer, journalist, and Washington correspondent before taking over the editorship of the 40,000-circulation monthly. Founded in 1909 by Robert M. LaFollette, Sr., the magazine consistently campaigned against militarism and, in more recent years, the nuclear arms race. More people "respected" than bought the magazine, and almost every year its editors had to solicit funds from loyal subscribers to keep going. It is published in Madison, only a few blocks from the former offices of *Kaleidoscope,* and in its own, more dignified (some say stuffy) way, it is every bit as antiestablishment as any underground paper.

In 1979 Knoll, along with his managing editor and an author, spent six months under federal court order not to publish a certain article or even to discuss its contents. They were neither the first nor the last journalists to be silenced by a judicial order, but none had ever been silenced for so long or so completely.

The author was Howard Morland, a freelance writer and antinuclear activist who wore his lack of scientific training like a badge. He had taken one science course in college, some years before. He argued that if he could uncover, understand, and convey this information, then surely it would be duck soup for the agent of any hostile nation. The article was called "The H-Bomb Secret: How We Got It, Why We're Telling It." It was written entirely from unclassified sources, but it did not tell how to build a hydrogen bomb, although that is the way it was often characterized both in the legal proceedings and in the press accounts. These three men were accused of paving the way for nuclear annihilation, and much of the press was hostile to them.

Morland, like most writers, argued with his editors about how to edit and present his findings, based on an extensive tour of nuclear facilities. Many of the visits were arranged by the federal government, and a large portion of his information came from the libraries at those facilities and interviews with government scientists. His most serious argument with Knoll was over the issue of sending the article to experts for review.

In his book, Morland (1981) insisted that the editors wanted a crackdown, thus attracting attention to the magazine and to the nuclear issue. At the time, Morland was less confident than they that the government would lose any court test on the secrecy issue. In any case, the editors sent the manuscript to some scientists, who in turn gave it to the government. The Justice Department quickly obtained a temporary order from a federal judge that prohibited the publication until a formal hearing could be set up. The legal issue had been joined.

It is important to stress that at no time did the government accuse the author or editors of stealing secret material; they did not need to, because a little-noticed provision of the Atomic Energy Act of 1946, passed when the United States enjoyed a brief monopoly on nuclear weaponry, asserted that all nuclear information was "restricted at birth." Although this incredibly broad claim had never been tested in court, it meant that such data are classified the minute they pop into someone's head.

While it lasted, the case was the most hotly debated prior restraint confrontation of this century; certainly it drew more attention than Near's case, and it was rivaled only by the government's attempt in 1971 to keep the New York *Times* and other newspapers from printing the *Pentagon Papers,* a history of American involvement in Vietnam.

The *Pentagon Papers* case (New York Times v. United States, 403 U.S. 713, 1971) was the first time (although not, as we shall see, the last) that the government attempted to impose prior restraints or to suggest the applicability of espionage laws to the mass media. The federal district judge, a former Office of Strategic Services officer himself, heard the case and was unconvinced by the government's arguments. He lifted the ban on publication, and the case moved at once to the Second Court of Appeals. Because the Supreme Court was winding down its term, the Appeals Court had only 72 hours to evaluate the 7,000 pages of the report and the conflicting claims of the newspapers and the government. The Appellate court voted to uphold the trial judge.

One of those appellate judges, James L. Oakes (1982) later admitted that a few of the items gave him pause, but that the government did not show that the publication would seriously endanger the nation's security. He believed that the government's indiscriminate overclassification of documents cast serious doubts on how vital the material was to national security. Permitting the publication, on the other hand, "allowed the positive good flowing in a democratic society from the free and open exchange of public and congressional communication about the whys and wherefores of our involvement in a war that nearly everyone—including perhaps even the executive branch—wanted ended. Involved in short was what the First Amendment prohibition was aimed at promoting: alerting the public to the duties of rulers."

The Supreme Court, in overturning the publication ban, suggested that a more dire emergency might justify prior restraint. That was the case the government was trying to make in its action against *The Progressive.*

Knoll (1981) described the Alice-in-Wonderland atmosphere of the case. Because he was not cleared to see secret documents, he could not participate effectively in his own defense. When his attorneys saw such materials, they were forbidden to discuss the contents with him. His attorneys submitted more than two dozen publications or broadcast transcripts containing the same allegedly "secret" material for which *The Progressive* was seeking permission. A Milwaukee reporter spent one week in public libraries and came up with the "secret." Edward Teller, "father of the hydrogen bomb," published much of the secret years before in an encyclopedia found in tens of thousands of American homes. At one point, Knoll's attorneys asked the judge to dismiss the suit. Not only did he decide to continue, but the reasons for his decision were themselves slapped with a classification of secret. As Knoll observed:

> All of these severe distortions of the judicial process help to illustrate why prior restraint has always been held in particular contempt by those who value freedom. Prior restraint is, perhaps, the most obnoxious form of governmental abuse because it puts the government's own conduct beyond public scrutiny. . . . The government needs to offer no public justification for imposing secrecy; the justification itself is secret.

At the conclusion of the hearing, Judge Robert Warren made the temporary order permanent. He admitted that he had not read the Morland article at the time of the first order, but he was willing to take the word of government officials for its pernicious character, an opinion he did not change after reading it and conducting the hearing. In issuing his temporary order, Warren used a line that haunted the defense for weeks and provided fodder for many hostile editorials and editorial cartoons: "I want to think a long, hard time before I'd give a hydrogen bomb to Idi Amin." Amin was then dictator of Uganda. Judge Warren later conceded that the article hardly "gave" a hydrogen bomb to anyone, since to build one, a nation needed an advanced scientific community and a vast industrial complex.

Think for a minute about the poor judge in such a case. All kinds of government officials tell him that the documents are absolutely vital to national security, that if he permits their public action, he will endanger world peace, if not the world itself. He has almost no one else to whom he can turn for advice. He is placed in precisely the same unenviable position as the censors, about whom we talked in earlier chapters. Like them, he must say "yes" or "no." Unlike a prosecutor employing some form of postrestraint, he does not have available the option of doing nothing and waiting to see what happens. He must act, and he must act in the name of the United States of America.

On March 26 Judge Warren made the ban permanent, relying on Hughes' suggestion in the Near decision that the First Amendment did not ban all prior restraints:

> What is involved here is information dealing with the most destructive weapon in the history of mankind, information of sufficient destructive potential to nullify the right to free speech and to endanger the right to life itself. . . . Faced with a stark choice between upholding the right to continue life and the right to freedom of the press, most jurists would have no difficulty in opting for the chance to continue to breathe and function as they work to achieve perfect freedom of expression.

Thus the judge set up the same kind of impossible "balancing test" that the state judge used in sentencing Mark Knops. Both concluded that free expression had to give way to asserted needs of the government to protect citizen safety. At least he conceded the article was not a do-it-yourself recipe for building a hydrogen bomb in the basement, because that required expensive and sophisticated factories and armies of trained scientists and technicians. Some editorial writers and cartoonists failed to make even that fundamental distinction.

An appeal was filed, and the fat was in the fire. *The Progressive's* small staff, augmented by volunteers, was overwhelmed with requests for interviews, speeches, and information. The telephones never stopped ringing and the legal costs never stopped mounting. "Our purpose, after all, had been to raise the issue of secrecy and to alert Americans to the awful peril of the nuclear arms race," Knoll wrote in the May 1979 issue of *The Progressive,* the one that was to have carried Morland's article. "The government had provided us with an opportunity to reach many more of our fellow citizens than we could ever hope to reach through the pages of this magazine. We were not about to let that opportunity go by. If we could not tell Morland's story about H-bomb secrecy, we could tell his story— and ours—about censorship and repression."

Initially, the reaction of much of the press toward *The Progressive* was negative. Some editors simply thought it was wrong to publish that kind of information; others worried that the appeal might give courts an opportunity to write an antipress decision with far-ranging repercussions. The Washington *Post,* for example, called it "a real First Amendment loser." The Chicago *Tribune,* along with the New York *Times* and the Boston *Globe,* were among the few consistent supporters of the challenge. The editor of *Harper's Magazine* expressed amazement "that both editors and lawyers seemed to presume that the First Amendment protected nice clean cases, but not awkward disputes."

As the weeks dragged by, attorneys working on the case in the Department of Justice urged the Attorney General to drop it, but it was a letter from a computer programmer to Senator Charles Percy that forced the issue. Charles Hansen described in detail what he had found out from unclassified documents about H-bomb construction; it was essentially the same things Morland had found and written about. He sent copies to eight newspapers, and the Madison *Press-Connection* printed Hansen's letter. The daily was published by striking employees of the other two dailies in the Wisconsin capital.

Although the Circuit Court of Appeals had not issued a decision on *The Progressive's* appeal, the Justice Department announced it would no longer enforce the ban. (Incidentally, Judge Warren never lifted his order, although it clearly was a meaningless relic.) Knoll published the article in his issue of November 1979, six months after he had intended.

Ironically, The Progressive did not profit financially from its months in the news. Although it sold a few extra thousand copies for awhile, its circulation at the end of six months was lower than at the beginning. The main reason was that its circulation staff had been too busy with appeals for funds to defray legal costs to dun subscribers. Although The Progressive incurred almost $250,000 in legal costs, it continued to publish, and no one doubted it would maintain its antiestablishment tone.

Looking back on the legal ordeal, Knoll (1981) said governmental claims of "national security" constitute the greatest threat to the First Amendment. If he had it to do over again, he said, he would publish the article and take his chances in court. Hughes's "narrow exception" in the Near decision ("no one would question that a government might prevent actual obstruction to its recruiting service or the publication of the sailing dates of transports or the number and location of troops") was the eye of the needle through which the government had brought the injunction against his magazine. Judge Warren had extended Hughes's wartime exception to times of peace.

In following the legal maneuverings, it is easy to lose sight of the nature of the materials in question. The newspapers were seeking to publish the Pentagon Papers at the very moment the national debate about American policy in Vietnam was being debated most broadly and most heatedly. They offered an unparalleled opportunity for the public to look over the shoulders of policymakers to see who had recommended what policy and for what reasons. Here was government policymaking of the past, but which vitally affected that moment, in the open. Certainly, that was not trivial. It allowed the public to form opinions on one of the most vital policies of their lifetime. It was information that was essential to political speech, the kind that had always been held in the highest esteem. So it was with the article enjoined from public attention in The Progressive. Anything having to do with national nuclear power is of vital concern to all citizens. People cannot hold informed opinions if they are banned from learning about it. Whether this was the best way to inform them is debatable; what is not debatable is that the government had no right to make that decision for the editors and for the public.

# 6

## "PROTECTORS" WHO SHAPED THE FIRST AMENDMENT

**Guardians—either elected or self-appointed—insist on legal protections for either the society at large or for children, in particular. Protections merge into restrictions.**

A classic cartoon shows a little old lady standing on the corner of a busy intersection and pounding a Boy Scout with her umbrella. "Good deed, hell! I didn't *want* to cross that street!" she is shouting.

Like the lady in the cartoon, many citizens do not want some of the protections enacted on their own behalf and are no more pleased with them when told they are "for your own good." Some well-intentioned protections either prove to be wrongheaded or, with changes in the world, inappropriate. Laws couched in terms of protecting women have come under serious question in recent years, as have some of those protecting children.

In the realm of the First Amendment, earlier chapters bristled with examples of intended protections that turned out to be the reverse. To cite only two, Congress granted those accused under the Sedition Act of 1798 the right to prove truth, but trial judges interpreted that to mean that every word in an issue of a newspaper had to be proved literally true, and those who would apply the logic of the "heckler's veto" to protect a provocative speaker from physical harm may keep him from speaking at all.

In this chapter, we will consider two major strands of protectionist arguments, one for guarding the nation from foreign influences and the other for shielding children from written and broadcast material.

### IMMIGRATION RESTRICTIONS

Every ordered society is fearful, or at least distrustful, of foreigners. Ancient Greece, for example, regarded all non-Greeks as uncivilized barbarians. In the Latin tongue, the concepts of "foreign" and "enemy" were contained in the same word. Every society treats aliens as having less than full rights.

Certainly, each American colony restricted who could settle there, and so did the new American government. The Nationalities Act, of four laws known collectively as the Alien and Sedition Laws, raised the period of residency before one could be naturalized to fourteen years, the longest in all our history. Why? Because many prominent Jeffersonians were recent arrivals from France or Ireland who brought with them their anti-British feelings. We saw in Chapter 2 that the Federalists identified closely with the British.

Although the waiting period was soon cut, it was only one in an unbroken series of attempts to fine-tune the immigration laws to favor certain nationalities and to limit or exclude others. Orientals have always been treated differently, and their special problems will be detailed separately below, but the vast majority came from Europe—first from the British Isles and northern Europe and then from southern and eastern Europe. Some fled political oppression, but most fled hard times. For example, one million Irish came during the 1840s because of the potato famine at home.

America's self-confidence can be measured in how wide it held open the immigration doors. Those doors began closing in the 1880s, and for all practical purposes they were bolted shut in the 1920s. By then, 50 million Europeans had pulled up stakes and sought their fortunes in this country. For the last 60 years, immigration has been a mere trickle, but at least the 1965 law eliminated the quotas based on race.

During the hard economic times of the 1880s, there were increasing demands to slow or curtail the flow of immigrants. Laborers, fearful for their jobs, and capitalists, frightened by riots and violent strikes in the coal fields and steel mills, were both vehement in their calls to Congress. And Congress responded with reductions in the total number of persons who could enter the country.

The turn-of-the-century immigration laws made it possible, for the first time, to deport someone who had entered the country illegally. They also established steps to keep out anarchists or even to deport those who later were convicted of anarchism. In practice, these were seldom invoked. From 1903 to 1921, the United States turned back 38 for holding anarchist beliefs and deported only 13. As "guests" in this country, the aliens had no recourse to American courts to appeal their fates. The Supreme Court in 1893 ruled that deportation was not a punishment but only an administrative process, and therefore not appealable (Preston, 1963).

In 1917, Congress overrode President Wilson's second veto to insert a literacy test into the requirements for entering the country and to permit deportation of any alien who advocated violence against the government. These insertions into the various immigration laws were the first federal sedition statutes since the Sedition Act of 1798.

## THE RED SCARE

In November 1919, and again two months later, Justice Department agents swooped down on public places and private homes to arrest at least 3000 aliens suspected of plotting the overthrow of the United States. The press, the citizenry, and Congress applauded the crackdown, considering it long overdue.

The summer of 1919 was a tense time in the nation. There was unemployment as the economy tried to readjust to peacetime conditions, and there were hundreds of strikes, some of them accompanied by violence. Letter bombs were mailed to public officials, and bombs were hurled at the homes of others (Murray, 1955). From the Soviet Union came a steady blare of boasts about worldwide revolution. Congress appropriated extra funds to the Attorney General, A. Mitchell Palmer, and told him pointedly to "do something" about the situation. Palmer, a former congressman and a leading candidate for the Democratic presidential nomination in 1920, laid his plans carefully for the alien raids.

Palmer declared that the time was past for trying to draw "nice distinctions . . . between the theoretical ideals of the radicals and their actual violations of our national law." His principal weapon was the change in the immigration laws, enacted during World War I, which outlawed anarchism in all its forms and permitted deportation of aliens who in any way violated the code. He interpreted that to mean even reading or receiving anarchist publications. Deportation hearings were swift and provided the aliens almost no legal protections (except in the extremely rare situation when a federal court issued a writ of habeas corpus and thus forced a fullblown trial). Otherwise, rulings of hearings officers were final.

Federal agents, augmented by local police, raided Russian centers in ten Eastern cities. Not only did they arrest 450 persons (several of them there to take night language courses), but they rummaged through files and carted off literature and records. More than half the Russians were released before the night was over, but by the next morning Palmer was a national hero. Quickly, Palmer secured deportation orders for 199 Russians who were found guilty of violating the immigration laws, and with 50 other deportees they were deported to Russia on the *Buford* in January.

Palmer was ready for greater victories. The solicitor in the Department of Labor agreed that it would no longer be necessary for arresting officers to inform aliens either of their right to counsel or of the specific charges against them. He also issued 3000 mimeographed warrants for the arrest of aliens whose names could be filled in before, during, or even after the raids.

There were raids in 33 cities on the night of 2 January 1919, and no one ever will know how many were arrested, since the records have disappeared. While almost all the press hailed the raids, local and national civil liberty organizations were alarmed and launched investigations. They found that the methods had been both ludicrous and appalling. In one city, police herded into jail everyone eating in a Russian restaurant and in another arrested an entire orchestra. In Detroit, more than 800 were arrested on half that many warrants. In other cities, those rounded up were jammed into makeshift quarters for days before being processed.

Perhaps the most damning report was issued four months after the January raids by a blue-ribbon committee of constitutional lawyers, including Zechariah Chafee, Jr. and Felix Frankfurter. It documented the illegal acts and the gross violations of civil liberties. At least two radicals were arrested solely because they had been photographed reading Russian-language newspapers and others because their names appeared on circulation lists of radical magazines. The committee insisted that such tactics endangered the democratic process far more than any alien plots.

Public and press support for Palmer ebbed quickly, and although he predicted massive uprisings on May Day and the Fourth of July, those days passed quietly. He promised thousands of aliens would be deported as a result of his January raids, but the "hanging jury" mood at the hearing boards had changed, and the deportation figure was 556. The Democratic convention delegates were afraid of his fading image and turned instead to the colorless Governor

James M. Cox of Ohio. Deportations for radicalism were over, but instead of focusing on getting rid of radicals, the makers and enforcers of federal policy threw their net wider and attempted to shut down immigration entirely.

The 1921 and 1924 immigration laws established a system of quotas based on nationality. Pegging this to the census figures of 1880 assured that the few immigrations would come from the "old stocks" of Britain and northern Europe and not from southern and eastern Europe. Scientists rushed forward with "proof" that the latter "races" were not assimilable into the American melting pot.

European immigration slowed to a trickle, and Orientals were barred entirely; however, Congress left loopholes permitting growers to continue bringing in vast numbers of seasonal laborers from Mexico.

While retaining the nationality quotas, the 1952 revision allowed the Justice Department to deport any alien already here who was involved in activities "prejudicial to the public interest" or "subversive to the national security." This was passed during the McCarthyism scare, as were bans on travel to communist countries and on receiving mail from those nations.

Finally, in 1965, Congress rejected the quota system, electing instead to set a limit on total immigration. Applicants from all nations would be considered for those spaces, and while the total figure was not large, it facilitated the entry of many from the Middle East and the Orient. There was a small wave of immigration from Vietnam following American military withdrawal from that nation.

### THE YELLOW PERIL

"The Yellow Peril" has been a persistent theme in American fiction as well as diplomacy. The term was first used as it applied to the flow of Chinese workers imported into this country in the late nineteenth century, many of them to build the railroads of the West. The Chinese were seen not only as "inscrutable" and exotic, but also as treacherous. When immigration laws at the end of the nineteenth century cut off this "threat," the anti-Oriental fears were shifted to the Japanese who were then coming to the United States.

The first naturalization act in 1790 provided that any alien "being a free white person" could be admitted to citizenship. The 1870 law enlarged this to include aliens of African nativity or descent, but it was 1922 before the Supreme Court was called upon to decide if the failure to mention Orientals and Hindus meant that they were not eligible. The court found that they were not. The timing of the decision cannot be overlooked, since it came in the midst of congressional efforts to close off immigration and when several Western states had barred Orientals from buying or owning land. (California courts did not find its exlusionary land law invalid until 1952.) Konvitz (1946) recounts the painful and unbroken pattern of legal discrimination against Orientals.

All of this served as background for what happened to Japanese Americans during World War II, one of the blackest marks in the history of American civil liberty. The imprisonment of 112,000 Japanese Americans (two-thirds of them citizens because they were born here) was justified officially on grounds of fears that the Japanese might invade the West Coast and would be aided by these persons. In its official history, the U.S. army admits that by the time the buses, trucks, and trains full of men, women, and children rolled out of West Coast cities in the spring of 1942, they had concluded that there was no real danger of invasion; however, the operation was already underway. The Supreme Court upheld the legality of the Executive Order banning the Japanese from the coast, and it did so on the grounds of the invasion danger. One of the dissenters called this opinion "a loaded gun" awaiting other minorities in future crises. The ACLU called the evacuation "the worst single wholesale violation of civil rights of American citizens in our history" and considered the Supreme Court's endorsement "one of the great failures in its history."

In the first days after Pearl Harbor, the FBI picked up and detained some 3600 enemy aliens, Japanese, Germans, and Italians. Investigations cleared almost all of them, and as rumors of a mass internment grew, the Justice Department announced that it could not handle the job. Finally, the War Department gave the West Coast army commander the power to evacuate the Japanese, but refused his request to include Germans and Italians as well. There were too many of them and they had too much political clout.

Several thousand Japanese Americans, reading the handwriting on the wall, moved eastward during the first three months, but at some state borders they were turned back by armed posses. In other cities they were made unwelcome. Still, those with families or marketable skills did manage to get to cities such as Chicago and

Detroit in reasonable numbers before such migration was cut off at the end of March 1942.

In Hawaii, 2400 miles nearer the fighting, there was no removal, although Japanese and Japanese Americans constituted more than one-third of the population. There were too many to move. There were also no cases of proven sabotage in Hawaii during the entire war.

Anti-Japanese feelings were fanned by their traditional opponents, the patriotic and farm groups of the West Coast. The Hearst press did its share, too. While the Japanese idled in the camps, groups such as the Native Sons and Daughters of the Golden West sought court orders to bar their return to California. Their logic was that those born in Japan could not become citizens and could not own land; therefore, they had entered the country illegally, which negated the claims of their American-born children to citizenship by reason of birth here. Such efforts failed, and eventually about half of those interned returned to California, while others spread throughout the nation, attracted by industrial and other kinds of jobs.

Magazines, newspapers, and congressmen frequently charged that the Japanese were being coddled in the camps, and while that charge was ludicrous, even the Japanese Americans admitted that those in charge did all that they could to be humane. Perhaps the best indication was that newspapers operated by internees in several centers were allowed to publish sharp criticisms of camp policies (Stevens, 1971).

After much soul searching, the government announced in early 1945 that the camps would be closed that summer. Many genuine humanitarians argued that the federal government had an obligation to take care of the people it had uprooted for as long as they wanted to stay, but those who prevailed warned about the possibility of establishing a new class of "Indian reservations" with its attendant evils. As it happened, the atomic bomb ended the war that summer, much earlier than expected.

However humane its administration, the internment was inexcusable, especially since it clearly was based on racial prejudice. Not only were Germans and Italians not interned, but the ACLU found little general harassment of them in cities across the nation, even in the depths of the war. Ten Broek et al. (1954) concluded that there was no other explanation for singling out the

Japanese except the belief that racial strains "remain undiluted through many generations and . . . are determinants of national loyalty." The belief in racial strains and loyalty certainly explains most of the history of American immigration policy.

## SPECIAL PROTECTIONS UNDER LAW

In the ancient area of law called "master-servant," the clear underpinning is paternalism: The wise master can best look after the interests of his servant (or slave). Although it is a concept born in the age of chivalry, it has been applied systematically in the modern age to the legal status of both women and children.

For a variety of reasons, most men in the early nineteenth century put women on pedestals, where they were admired as ornamental but not taken seriously. This was at that very time that women were playing such key roles in the campaign to abolish slavery. They were to be disappointed when in the post-Civil War amendments they were not extended, as were the former slaves, the right to vote and to be treated as equals.

During the nineteenth century, more and more women were drawn into the factory system, with its attendant health and safety horrors. Conditions were bad for both men and women, but the men found some voice through the unions, which for the most part were closed to women workers.

In 1908 the Supreme Court upheld an Oregon law to limit the hours of women's work. The decision was hailed as a great victory; however, in its wording and rationale, the decision rested on the traditional assumption of female inferiority: "She is properly placed in a class by herself, and legislation designed for her protection may be sustained, even when like legislation is not necessary for men and could not be sustained" (Muller v. Oregon, 208 U.S. 412). While the decision spurred the passage of hours, safety, and wage laws in most states, its logic came back 70 years later to haunt those working for the Equal Rights Amendment.

Although women could finally vote in federal elections after 1920, other progress came slowly. One court decision after another upheld laws barring women from certain occupations or positions. They were guaranteed equal pay for equal work by the Equal Pay Act of 1963 and the Civil Rights Act of 1964, but four-fifths were employed in "women's jobs" that had no direct male counterparts.

In 1982 the Supreme Court endorsed the much broader idea of equal pay for *comparable* jobs, thus opening new vistas for clericals and others confined to traditional ghettoes of female work.

Of course, not all women objected to their special status. Many were prominent in campaigns against liberalized abortion laws and the Equal Rights Amendment. There always have been and always will be those who enjoy being protected.

Americans have been even more eager to protect children, but not until recently to protect them from the almost total control by parents or those institutions who stand in for parents. The very concept of "adolescence" as a distinct phase of a lifetime, tucked in between childhood and adulthood, dates from the last two decades of the nineteenth century. With the decreasing demand for child labor in factories and the corresponding availability of secondary schools, older children were defined into this legal purgatory. Western nations generalized the age-old problem of juvenile crime (remember Dickens's novels of a half-century earlier) into the broader one of juvenile delinquency. Later studies have shown that there were no more youths arrested for such crimes as theft and assault during that era than in the ones before or after; rather, policemen were more likely to pick up idling youths, and teachers and parents were more willing to turn to courts for help in controlling incorrigible children.

While earlier arguments for protecting children were moral and religious, at the turn of the century they became "scientific." Reformers (many of them Darwinians much impressed with determinism) wanted to apply science to child rearing. Presumably, society had such a stake in the way its children turned out that their rearing could not be left strictly to parents. Laws, however, continued to recognize that parents, for all practical purposes, "owned" their children.

American and European lawmakers enacted laws to protect children, as they had women, from the excesses of the industrial revolution: long hours, low wages, and safety hazards. By the time these laws were enacted, however, the demand for child labor in factories had already dropped substantially. Other laws protected children by penalizing those who sold them liquor, cigarettes, or obscene materials.

One of the most noteworthy accomplishments of Progressive reformers was the establishment of juvenile courts, with their attendant penal and reform systems. The common law had been harsh. Those 7 to 14 years, if they understood what they had done, were tried as adults, as were all those over that age. No longer would adolescents be tried in the same courts or held in the same prisons as hardened adult criminals. The goal of the juvenile courts was leniency. Justice would be individualized. The judges, instead of being bound by the formalities and rules of evidence, would listen to social workers and parents, as well as police, and then act on behalf of the children. As a further protection, there would be no permanent record to haunt them in later life, and juvenile court proceedings would be kept secret.

Well-intentioned though they were, these protections were attained at a high price. Juvenile defendants had virtually no procedural safeguards and were almost never represented by counsel. Without counsel, appeals are virtually impossible, even when it can be shown that sentences for the same offense vary wildly from judge to judge and even from case to case. This is precisely what the Supreme Court said in 1967. The court told the states that their juvenile courts went too far, and in their zeal to protect youthful offenders had actually prevented fair trials. Defendants were entitled to counsel and were to be protected from self-incrimination and related evils.

In another decision, the court ruled that states cannot prohibit the publication of the name of a juvenile offender. If newspapers or stations can get the name, they can use it. Most media do not publish or broadcast such names by policy, and there was no rush to do so in the aftermath of the decision, but they wanted it to be their option to decide whether certain juvenile offenders needed protecting.

Paul Goodman (1960) focused public attention on the restrictions that law, tradition, and families place on American children, and in the two decades since there have been many legal challenges to using age as a criterion, either for special treatment or for judging competence. The results have been mixed. Research that has attempted to measure attitudes on the rights of children has found little consensus. For example, Bohrnstedt et al. (1981) concluded, after attaining adult responses to a series of vignettes that dramatized such questions, that any proponents of change in the area of parent-child rights—regardless of which direction they wanted to go—were going to run into a sizable opposition. Society is deeply divided on these fundamental issues.

Even the Children's Defense Fund, one of the most vocal child advocacy groups, stated in 1978: "Children are not adults. They have special needs and are dependent in many ways on the care of adults and institutions. CDF believes children should be extended rights in some instances, especially where arbitrariness or discrimination are likely to occur or where the denial of a right may have serious consequences." That is hardly the language of absolutism.

In many areas of law, the age of majority is still in question. Eighteen-year-olds have been able to vote in federal elections since 1970, but in many states they need parental permission to marry and must submit to special restrictions about entering into contracts, holding certain jobs, and purchasing alcohol. The public is still ambivalent about how much protection it should provide its youth. In no area is this more true than in obscenity.

## PROTECTING CHILDREN FROM OBSCENITY

Plato would have banished poets from his ideal Republic. While he worried some about the false ideas they might spread among adults, his primary concern was in protecting youth from corruption. Plato would have orchestrated every facet of life to mold the youth into the kind of useful citizen that the society wanted. Poems, partly because they were attractive and fun, could impede that process.

Throughout history, most arguments for suppressing obscene, violent, or dangerous materials have been posed in terms of protecting children. Every community has assumed a special protection for the health and safety of its children; protection of morals is a logical extension. Some argue that adults manage to avoid coming to grips with their own feelings about the materials by arguing about the effects on children, but whatever the motivation, the roots are ancient. Modern societies assume two types of special responsibility toward children: shielding them from adult exploitation and assisting their growth and maturation. Arguments for controls on print, film, and broadcast material have been based on both rationales.

We will turn first to the control of obscenity. Most important American obscenity laws and court decisions have turned, directly or indirectly, on the protection of children.

The English definition, known as the Hicklin rule, was adopted in the late nineteenth century by American as well as British courts, and it stood rock solid until 1934. That rule defined obscene material as that which tended "to deprave and corrupt those whose minds are open to such immoral influences and into hands a publication of this sort might fall."

While the definition did not mention children, it was clearly women, children, and to a lesser degree, servants and members of the lower classes that the judges had in mind. The ruling came at a period when the impact of widespread literacy was being felt and women were the major users of fiction. There had been much less worry about Fielding's bawdy novels when they had circulated only among urbane males. Although the New England Puritans tried to suppress "idle" as well as suggestive books, sexy pictures circulated in colonial America, and Benjamin Franklin penned some of the best-known and privately circulated risque essays. Some delegates to the Constitutional Convention probably passed the sultry summer evenings reading these essays. These men knew England had been regulating obscene materials for half a century, yet they never even discussed regulating it here.

Why were they so blasé? Perhaps because bawdy prints and essays circulated only among the "better class" males like themselves, and *they* could not be corrupted by such feeble stuff. Elitists before and since have worried only when "dangerous" materials fall into the hands of the poor, the ignorant, and above all, women and children.

The man who shaped American obscenity law was Anthony Comstock, who warred on obscenity from 1872 until his death in 1915. Not only did he organize a powerful antivice society, but he lobbied through both the federal and New York statutes. In his most famous book, *Traps for the Young* (1883/1967), he revealed Satan's tactics:

And it came to pass that as Satan went to and fro upon the earth, watching his traps and rejoining over his numerous victims, he found room for improvement in some of his schemes. The daily press did not meet all his requirements. The weekly illustrated papers of crime would do for young men and sports, for brothels, gin-mills, and thieves' resorts, but were found to be so gross, so libidinous, so monstrous, that every decent person spurned them. They were excluded from the home on sight. They were too high-priced for children, and too cumbersome to be conveniently hid from the parent's eye or carried in the boy's pocket. So he resolved to make another trap for boys and girls especially.

He also resolved to make the most of these vile illustrated weekly papers, by lining the news-stands and shopwindows along the pathway of the children from home to school and church, so that they could not go to and from these places of instruction without giving him opportunity to defile their pure minds by flaunting these atrocities before their eyes.

And Satan rejoiced greatly that professing Christians were silent and apparently acquiesced in his plans.

Satan stirred up certain of his willing tools on earth by the promise of a few paltry dollars to improve greatly on the death-dealing quality of the weekly death-traps, and forthwith came a series of new snares of fascinating construction, small and tempting in price, and baited with high-sounding names. These sure-ruin traps comprise a large variety of half-dime novels, five and ten cent story papers, and low-priced pamphlets for boys and girls.

This class includes the silly, insipid tale, the coarse, slangy story in the dialect of the barroom, the blood-and-thunder romance of border life, and the exaggerated details of crimes, real and imaginary. Some have highly colored sensational reports of real crimes, while others, and by far the larger number, deal with most improbable creations of fiction. The unreal far outstrips the real. Crimes are gilded, and lawlessness is painted to resemble valor, making a bid for bandits, brigands, murderers, thieves, and criminals in general. Who would go to the State prison, the gambling saloon or the brothel to find a suitable companion for the child? Yet a more insidious foe is selected when these stories are allowed to become associates for the child's mind and to shape and direct the thoughts.

The finest fruits of civilization are consumed by these vermin. Nay, these products of corrupt minds are the eggs from which all kinds of villainies are hatched. Put the entire batch of these stories together, and I challenge the publishers and vendors to show a single instance where any boy or girl has been elevated in morals, or where any noble or refined instinct has been developed by them.

The leading character in many, if not in the vast majority of these stories, is some boy or girl who possesses unusually extraordinary beauty of countenance, the most superb clothing, abundant wealth, the strength of a giant, the agility of a squirrel, the cunning of a fox, the brazen effrontery of the most daring villain, and who is utterly destitute of any regard for the laws of God or man. Such a one is foremost among desperadoes, the companion and beau-ideal of maidens, and the high favorite of some rich person, who by his patronage and endorsement lifts the young villain into lofty positions in society, and provides liberally of his wealth to secure him immunity for his crimes. These stories link the pure maiden with the most foul and loathsome criminals. Many of them favor violation of marriage laws and cheapen female virtue.

The Supreme Court did not review the obscenity issue until 1957, when in striking down a Michigan law barring distribution to the general public of materials that might incite a minor to "violent or depraved or immoral acts," it insisted that no law could limit all readers in order to shield the innocence of juveniles (Butler v. Michigan, 352 U.S. 380). In all of its decisions since, the court has been careful to exclude pornography from the protection of the First Amendment and has concentrated instead on adjusting the boundaries where pornography and other speech meet. It has been many years since a court has found a book pornographic on the basis of printed descriptions alone; those materials defined as obscene have been all or partly graphics.

In its landmark Roth v. United States (354 U.S. 476) decision in 1957, the Supreme Court pulled together the phrases from various lower court opinions to define obscenity: "whether to the average person applying contemporary community standards the work taken as a whole appeals to prurient interest." In subsequent decisions the court allowed the states to set their own standards, so long as they stayed within this general framework. Most prosecutors decided to wink at adult bookstores and movie theaters, so long as they kept children out and did not thrust their wares on unsuspecting adults. Sometimes they gave into local pressures, just as did public or school librarians or, for that matter, Pontius Pilate.

In Bantam Books v. Sullivan (372 U.S. 58, 1963), the Supreme Court overturned a commission set up by Rhode Island "to educate the public concerning any book . . . or other thing containing obscene, indecent or impure language, or manifestly tending to the corruption of youth." The commission did this by sending booksellers lists of books objectionable for minors and asking them not to stock them. The notices reminded the booksellers that prosecutions might follow, since the lists had also been sent to local police officials. The Supreme Court found the practice unconstitutional, adding, "We are not the first court to look through forms to the substance and recognize that informal censorship may sufficiently inhibit the circulation of publications to warrant injunctive relief."

Five years later, the court invalidated a New York statute on the grounds of vagueness. It had prohibited the sale of any magazine that would "appeal to the lust of persons under the age of 18 years or to their curiosity as to sex or to the anatomical differences between the sexes."

In 1968 the Supreme Court addressed itself at length to the thorny issue of limiting sales of obscene materials to minors, materials that would not be obscene if sold to adults. A New York statute made it unlawful to sell to anyone under the age of 17 any picture depicting "nudity, sexual conduct or sado-masochistic abuse and which is harmful to minors," or any book or printed material with similar material "or explicit or detailed verbal descriptions" of the same. The definitions were precise. For example, nudity meant showing "human male or female genitals, pubic area or buttocks with less than a full opaque covering of any portion thereof below the top of the nipple, or the depiction of covered male genitals in a discernibly turgid state."

The operator of a Long Island luncheonette was convicted under the statute for selling two girlie magazines to a 16-year-old boy. The Supreme Court upheld his conviction (Ginsberg v. New York, 391 U.S. 629), although the magazines were not obscene for adults. The state could set such limits, and the youth had no constitutional right to obtain the material. The court cited a long series of interpretations recognizing parents' claim to authority for moral training and found this law in that tradition. It also reiterated the state's own interest in the well-being of its youth. It quoted approvingly from another decision:

While the supervision of children's reading may best be left to their parents, the knowledge that parental control or guidance cannot always be provided and society's transcendant interest of protecting the welfare of children justify reasonable regulation of the sale of material to them. It is, therefore, altogether fitting and proper for a state to include in a statute designed to regulate the sale of pornography to children special standards, broader than those

embodied in legislation aimed at controlling dissemination of such
material to adults.

After surveying the research and conducting some studies of its
own, the National Commission on Obscenity and Pornography
(1970) concluded that delinquent and nondelinquent youths first
saw erotic materials at about the same age and used them about as
frequently. They were neither more nor less stimulated by them.
In one poll conducted by the commission, two-thirds of adults
said they believed that "sexual materials excited people sexually,"
but only 15 percent said they had such an effect on themselves,
personally. Similarly, three-fifths agreed that such material
provided information about sex, and more than half thought they
provided entertainment for others; however, for themselves, the
figures were less than 20 percent. Somewhat more than half
thought such sexual materials contributed to a breakdown in
morals, but only 1 percent thought they had such an effect on
themselves. As we saw in earlier chapters, people are always
concerned about "protecting" others, the more susceptible, but
almost never express any worry about themselves.

Child protection was at the heart of the 1978 Supreme Court
decision to uphold the FCC's ban on "indecent" speech. A New
York City radio station, in presenting an hour-long program one
afternoon on the power of words, played a 12-minute cut from a
record by comedian George Carlin. Carlin was talking about the
seven words (all referring to sex or excretion) that could not be used
on the air, and of course in the process used all seven repeatedly.
The station had broadcast a warning to the faint-hearted to turn
their dials, but one man, riding in his car with his 15-year-old son,
heard the monologue and complained to the FCC. The commission
merely slapped the wrist of the station but issued an order banning
those words during hours when children are most likely to hear
them. The commission said it was not censoring but merely
"channeling" the words into late-night listening hours. The station
said Carlin was not "mouthing obscenities" but satirizing attitudes
toward those words, so it appealed to the courts.

Five years after the material was aired, the Supreme Court said
that the FCC could regulate "indecent" speech, even if the material
did not meet the legal definition of obscenity. The same
monologue that might be protected speech in a theater, on the
screen of a movie house, on a phonograph record played in the

privacy of a home, or printed in a magazine was subject to special restrictions if it was played over the public airwaves.

Here the court was dealing with a vital issue, because broadcast licensing has been justified by the shortage argument. There were not enough airwaves for everyone, so those granted the use of these valuable public resources must accept certain restrictions for the privilege. Technology now threatens that logic. Videotapes and videodiscs play and record. Satellites and laser systems broadcast directly into homes without using lines. Videotex systems bring words to the TV screen. Cable delivery systems multiply the number of stations received in each community. Rather than shortage, the future may hold excess.

The Supreme Court sidestepped the shortage rationale and cited two other reasons for regulating broadcasting more than print media. First, broadcast media are uniquely pervasive. The material invades the privacy of the home, "where the individual's right to be let alone plainly outweighs the First Amendment rights of an intruder." Prior warnings are not enough, because the audience is changing constantly. Second, broadcasting is "uniquely accessible" to children, even those too young to read. The Court added, "[such a] broadcast could have enlarged a child's vocabulary in an instant." (Perhaps the justices underestimate the age at which children pick up such worlds.) The majority opinion cited approvingly an earlier justice's remark that a "nuisance may be merely a right thing in the wrong place—like a pig in the parlor instead of in the barnyard."

Justice William Brennan, in a forceful dissent, insisted that the federal government had only the power to regulate the obscene. As for children, this material did not appeal to their prurient interests. He insisted that what the courts consistently upheld was the right of parents, not the government, to regulate the activities of children:

As surprising as it may be to individual Members of this Court, some parents may actually find Mr. Carlin's unabashed attitude towards the seven "dirty words" healthy, and deem it desirable to expose their children to the manner in which Mr. Carlin defuses the taboo surrounding the words. Such parents may constitute a minority of the American public, but the absence of great numbers willing to exercise the right to raise their children in this manner does not alter the right's nature or its existence. Only the Court's regrettable decision does that.

Leaving aside the problem of whether it is possible to distinguish what is dangerous for adults and youths to read and view, there are many who argue that the attempt should not be made, precisely because it confirms youthful distrust of adults and reinforces the concept of a distinct youthful subculture. If alienation is a major problem in the generation gap, then surely this contributes to it.

The movies present another area where censorship has been based on arguments for protecting youth. Early social workers were appalled at the filthy conditions in the cheap movie houses and by the amount of time children were spending in these dark, unsupervised environs, often watching films about crime. Several cities used health laws to try to control movie houses. The antimovie attitude played some unspecified part in the Supreme Court's decision in 1915 that motion pictures were not protected by the First Amendment. They remained so until 1952, but of course by then the movies had broadened their age and class appeal.

Cities and states set up their own boards to approve films before they could be shown, and while the Supreme Court consistently held these boards to tough procedural safeguards, it always refused to ban them on any constitutional ground. Slowly they became anachronisms, and in 1981 Maryland allowed its review board to die. It was the last one in the country.

The movie industry established its own rating system in 1968 to keep the government from doing the same thing. These ratings have no legal power; they are only advisory to theater owners and parents. They are based primarily on the explicitness of sex. Parents tell opinion pollers they want tougher standards, and few of them attend movies. More than three-fourths of regular moviegoers are under 25, and a substantial share are under 17.

Theaters that show explicit sex films give ample warnings about the nature of their fare through their ads (where the newspapers will run them), their marquees, and their premium prices. No one is likely to walk in off the street expecting to see a Walt Disney double feature, and ticket sellers often insist on proof of age. Many of these theaters are owned by chains that budget money to fight local obscenity prosecutions as one of their normal costs of doing business. Often they win, but the Supreme Court has held that these theaters can be prosecuted under local ordinances, even if they give ample warning and are careful to ban children.

One particularly tawdry brand of material has drawn special attention from lawmakers in recent years. That is so-called "kiddie porn." Several states have enacted laws aimed at those who exploit children to pose for either still or motion pictures. Most civil libertarians find it difficult to defend the makers of such stuff with much vigor, although a First Amendment absolutist would have to. So far, no one convicted under "kiddie porn" law has used the plea that his material is not obscene because it does not have prurient appeal for the "average person" but only for pederasts. A few years ago, the Supreme Court rejected that same line of defense offered for a publisher of magazines directed toward masochists.

## PROTECTING CHILDREN FROM VIOLENT CONTENT

Adults in all societies have tended to conclude that anything that attracts children must somehow be evil. At best it is a time killer; at worst, it is a corrupter. It is an unbroken line from the poems of ancient Greece to the rock music and electronic games of today. In between have come pantomimes, shoot-em-up novels and story papers, pulp magazines, movies, comic books, and inevitably, television.

Congressional concern about television violence dates back to 1954 when network officials assured the Senate Subcommittee on Juvenile Delinquency that research on effects were "mixed" and that they were busy conducting more studies. The subcommittee received similar assurances in 1961 and 1964, as did hearings before the National Commission on the Causes and Prevention of Violence in 1968. The Surgeon General's commission concluded flatly that there was a causal relationship between viewing televised violence and subsequent antisocial behavior in a substantial number of children.

Considering how much television content is violent (the average child is alleged to have witnessed 13,000 violent deaths on the tube by the time he graduates from high school), it is not surprising that there have been demands to do something to curb it. Throughout most of its history, the Federal Communications Commission has tried to avoid any decisions that involve dictating program content, since such decisions inevitably run into First Amendment difficulties.

But the critics would not be put off so easily. The first line of argument was the traditional one that those who view antisocial behavior will go out and emulate it. The second is more subtle. It suggests that watching this kind of behavior tends to desensitize viewers, to make them more nervous and less trusting. Of course, by "viewers," most critics mean children. As with pornography, most people are not worried about what it might do to themselves.

What does the research say? After reviewing 67 published studies, a Canadian sociologist concluded that regardless of method of measurement or age of children studied, the preponderance of evidence points toward a correlation between viewing violent TV or film fare and increased aggression (Andison, 1977). But social science findings do not dictate policy; they merely provide one of several kinds of input that policymakers need. Because of vast individual differences, there is a serious question whether laws can or should try to impose content standards. Dorr and Kovarik (1980), unlike many social science researchers, have pointed out the First Amendment issues and urged caution in approaching regulation of content.

The FCC chairman, in an effort to reduce the amount of violence in prime-time television, pressured the networks into accepting the so-called family viewing hour policy. The idea was to relegate programs with more adult themes to later time slots, presumably when fewer young children would be watching. The networks reluctantly complied, but the Writers Guild, believing that the chairman had used undue "persuasion" and in doing so had limited what they could write about, went to court and had the policy nullified.

By the age of three or four, many children spend most of their waking hours in front of a glowing tube. Most of what they see was produced primarily for adults. Yale University researchers found the pacing and tone of a program—quite aside from its ostensible theme—was what correlated with aggressive behavior among viewers in selected nursery schools. Aggression was induced about as much by watching the winners on game shows jump up and down and scream or by situation comedies with lots of screaming as by police and detective programs (Singer and Singer, 1979). The Canadian media observer, Marshall McLuhan, suggested many years ago that it was the medium, not the message, that really mattered. The Yale studies would tend to substantiate his claim.

It seems ironic that the same parents who want the government to "do something" about what their children see on the TV screen refuse to supervise it in their own homes. Lyle and Hoffman (1972) found that only one-third of parents even claimed to try to control the amount and type of shows their children watched. One wonders how they expect some government agency to accomplish what they cannot, to make wiser decisions for the diverse families of the nation if they refuse to make them for their own.

Much research has tried to discover links between what children watch on the tube and what they do to emulate it. One of the clearest findings, however, is that many more children model their *viewing behavior* after what they see in their homes. If their parents watch lots of TV and do it fairly indiscriminately, then the children almost certainly will do the same. Modeling, like charity, begins at home (O'Bryant and Corder-Bolz, 1978).

Not all complaints have focused on sex and violence. There have also been demands for more program variety and for limits on TV advertising directed at children. As for variety, G. Comstock (1980) suggests that the long history of FCC efforts shows the agency's importance in program regulation. In 1974, the FCC called on stations and networks to schedule more "age-specific" programming and to spread it throughout the week. Five years later, a study found little compliance, and the FCC simply shrugged. In 1979, the FCC chairman repeated the traditional pleas to the broadcasters, urging them to clean up their acts before the government did it for them. Such classic expressions of social responsibility theory were heard no more from his successor. In the 1980s, the mood of deregulation was so overwhelming that no one in authority even paid such lip service to concepts such as forcing improvements in children's programming.

During the 1970s, the Federal Trade Commission seemed to be interested in regulating TV advertising aimed at young viewers. The FTC has general responsibility for prohibiting false and misleading advertising of all types. In 1978, its staff recommended a total ban on advertising aimed at very young viewers and severe limits on ads for sugared products directed at older children. Since manufacturers of sugar-coated cereals and candy products are among the largest advertisers on existing children's shows, and since the problems in defining the age boundaries proved so onerous, the issue died without being enacted into law. The new members of the FTC, appointed by the Reagan Administration, have shown no interest in renewing the inquiries.

# 7

# PRINT TECHNOLOGY AND
# THE FIRST AMENDMENT

**Printing brought with it not only the ability to spread sedition
and blasphemy but also to damage reputations and infringe
on works created by others.**

Political and religious leaders started worrying seriously about
"dangerous" ideas only when they could be transmitted efficiently
to masses of people. Such dangers were minimal when each
message had to be chiseled in stone or copied painstakingly by
hand, but the printing press changed that. Suddenly, the potential
for mischief was multiplied first by a hundredfold and eventually by
a millionfold. There were immediate steps to control the presses,
just as there would be later to control each emerging technology
that improved communication.

Handwritten newsletters had circulated since the days of Rome,
and by the time of the development of printing from movable type
in Europe in the fifteenth century, there were organized
commercial services that circulated such newsletters to far-flung
businessmen, soldiers, public officials, and clerics. Since they were
costly, their circulation was limited to the elites. Obscene materials
also circulated from hand to hand.

Printing arrived just in time to ride the crest of inquisitiveness in
all areas—religious, scientific, and governmental. Printing spread
these new ideas too efficiently for the taste of many in power. Such
tight controls were clamped on the presses that it was a century and
a half before a newspaper appeared.

## PRIOR RESTRAINT

Each government required that before a printer could produce
copies of any work, he had to submit it for official approval. The
censor could refuse and was not required to give his reasons. The
printer who published anyway did so at his own peril. This system
provided absolute control until there were too many printers

operating or until sizable amounts of printed matter could be imported. Economic determinists have explained the breakdown as a matter of presses having unused capacity, but that explanation is too simple-minded. There was a whole change in the relationship between citizens and all institutions, and the printing press not only was an agent of that change but a beneficiary of it (Eisenstein, 1978). The governments worried about the spread of sedition and the churches about the spread of heresy. Although literacy was still limited, it was far higher than it had been before the advent of printing.

Battles over freedom of the press for the first two centuries after the introduction of printing centered on prior restraints. With each passing decade, these controls became less efficient and less popular. In 1695 England became the first European nation to end prior censorship (although the monarchs invented all sorts of postpublication controls).

America's settlement and most of its colonial experience took place under British tradition and rule; however, for reasons outlined in the first chapter, prior censorship was eliminated a half-century earlier in the American colonies than at home.

France and Germany kept prior censorship of the press until about a century ago; it is still the rule in most one-party states. Although American courts are suspicious of any licensing scheme that touches on the First Amendment, they have upheld the licensing of broadcasting stations and the right of local boards of review to license films. They also permit local officials to issue permits for parades, meeting rooms, and rallies (see Chapter 4, this volume). But they have refused to countenance licensing or permit schemes for printed materials, even when officials have argued that leafleting contributes to littering or traffic congestion. If those problems occur, the court has said, they are the price of unimpeded communication. Although the justices never say it quite so bluntly (for understandable reasons), it is clear that print has a preferred position in the pantheon of First Amendment protections.

There are three areas of law that have been shaped in large part by print materials: obscenity, copyright, and libel.

## OBSCENITY AND BLASPHEMY

In the last chapter we disussed obscenity as a protectionist concept. There are other aspects. Obscenity law emerged from theological, not legal, precepts. For centuries, it was the church, not the state, that was concerned about the dangers from ideas and words. Printing accelerated those fears. Obscenity law is anchored in blasphemy, or abuse of the gods. (One Roman emperor reportedly told an official demanding punishment of an alleged blasphemer that if the gods were offended, then the gods should do their own punishing. But not everyone was so willing to trust the gods.)

Blasphemy slowly disappeared from American law, the Supreme Court delivering the coup de grace in 1952 when it refused to allow the Chicago film board to ban a film because it was sacrilegious. The Italian film depicted a demented peasant woman's claims that her illegitimate child was fathered by St. Joseph. Prosecutions for printed blasphemy had been abandoned far earlier.

In the area of modern obscenity law, that is, prosecutions for lewdness, printed words became much safer after the 1935 decision in the *Ulysses* case. Among other things, that decision established that a work must be considered in its entirety. No longer could prosecutors convict by picking out individual words and phrases; with all the modifications in the half-century since, that principle has stood rock solid.

Author Gore Vidal, in his 1974 novel, *Myron*, used satire to show that what most bluenoses objected to was the context, and not the offensive words themselves. He did this by substituting for the usual "dirty" words the names of Supreme Court justices and antismut campaigners. He explained in the preface that he hoped this would keep people from "burgering" around with the language.

Of course, the same press that prints words can also reproduce drawings and photographs, either to accompany the words or to stand by themselves. To convict even the sleaziest magazine or book of obscenity, the prosecutor must show that the predominant appeal of the entire issue—pictures and words together—is to prurient interest. Courts sometimes do uphold convictions, especially when they conclude that the words are there only as an excuse for publishing obscene photos. Perhaps the most interesting case was the publisher who reprinted the text of the Obscenity Commission report (clearly of public importance and clearly not within the definition of the obscene), but illustrated with photographs, explicit in the extreme. The Supreme Court upheld the conviction.

Courts have consistently held that obscene materials are not protected by copyright, but that is only one of the First Amendment issues involved in that complex area of law.

## COPYRIGHT

Copyright was conceived as a protection for the property rights of authors. Article I, Section 8 of the Constitution empowers Congress to "promote the progress of science and useful arts, by securing for limited times to authors and inventors the exclusive right to their respective writings and discoveries." The first law of 1790 protected only books, maps, and charts, but during the next 75 years, musical compositions, dramatic performances, and photographs were added. The Copyright Law of 1909 gave limited protection to phonograph records and set off endless court battles on that aspect. In 1954 the Supreme Court held that copyright protected pictoral, graphic, or sculptured works, even when they were employed in the design of useful articles. With the rise of gigantic record, motion picture, and broadcasting industries, the inadequacies of the 1909 law became ever more obvious; however, it was 1976 before a comprehensive revision was enacted.

But let us return to the print media. American book publishers refused to sign the international copyright agreement of 1837 because they subsisted on the profits from publishing fiction by British authors. Why pay for it when they could pirate it? Eventually, to control competition among themselves, they worked out an intricate pattern of gentlemen's agreements. They would pay British publishers something for "pirating rights" and respect prior claims by other American publishers. These fell apart in later competitive book wars, and Americans signed the new international pact in 1891. (Russia and many other communist nations still have not signed.)

Although the 1976 revision retained the philosophical underpinnings of earlier copyright law, several substantial changes were made. For example, the period of copyright was extended from 14 years plus a renewal of 14 years to the lifetime of the author plus 50 years. It also wiped out a patchwork of state copyright laws and reserved the area exclusively for the federal government. The law established a system of compensation for owners of music played on other media and a system of payment to producers of television programs by cable operators.

The 1976 copyright law states emphatically that ideas or concepts are not copyrightable, but the expressions of the ideas or concepts are. Courts have found infringements where there have been paraphrases, additions, and omissions, so there is more to the test than its verbatim nature. The line is not a formula but an application in each instance to the balance between what the second version has added or abstracted from the first. In a classic example, a wire service lost its claims to copyrightability of news of an event, even when it had the only reporter on the scene, assuming other media or services added research, details, or substantially altered the report.

Nimmer (1980) sees an inevitable conflict between the concepts of free expression and of copyrightability. Courts have consistently held that the First Amendment protects nearly everything that a speaker says or a writer writes, not just those parts that are original with him or her. Copyright, on the other hand, is concerned only with the original parts of the presentation. He found that the courts had carefully avoided this fundamental issue, but added, "One can predict with confidence, however, that such a confrontation will eventually occur."

## DEFAMATION

If courts have not dealt with that fundamental issue, they certainly have been dealing for a long time with alleged damages to reputations. Gossip and innuendo are as old as man. As soon as we could grunt, we were probably telling tales on our neighbors; as soon as we could tell stories with pictures, we were probably telling none-too-nice ones. But there was a difference. When we made our accusations orally, there was no permanent record, but when we began to paint or chip them in stone, they were there for others to see.

It was the permanence and the multiplied capacity for doing damage that led to the legal distinctions between slander (oral) and libel (written) defamation. Although they emerged from separate legal traditions, they are virtually indistinguishable today. It took courts decades to conclude that defamation broadcast over the radio was more like libel than slander; once they did, the remaining distinctions (having to do mostly with the types of damages) became too technical for us to worry about here.

The law of defamation seeks to protect individual reputations from false and injurious remarks. It grew up in criminal law, but today it is almost exclusively a matter of civil law. Under criminal law, it was designed to prevent attacks on the government and its leaders (commonly called seditious libel) or breach of the peace. A British court in 1606 ruled:

> If it be against a private man it deserves mere punishment, for although the libel be made against one, yet it incites all those of the same family, kindred, or society to revenge, and so tends . . . to quarrels and breach of the peace, and may be the cause of shedding of blood, and of great inconvenience; if it be against a magistrate, or other public person, it is a greater offence; for it concerns not only the breach of the peace, but also the scandal of Government.

There are interesting assumptions in this decision of nearly four centuries ago. It makes the distinction between public and private figures that is still at the heart of libel. Today, however, we have reversed the priorities. The decision stresses the possible social evils resulting from libels and assumes that prompt and strong legal actions will deter vigilante actions.

There was a time when defamers were dealt with directly and harshly. In seventeenth-century England, judges not only fined and imprisoned them, but they sometimes had them whipped or their ears cut off. One man arrested in 1640 had already had his ears cut off for a previous libel conviction, so he was branded on the forehead.

Criminal libel had a long and distasteful history as a protector for those who already had too much power. (One need only recall the Zenger trial and the experiences under the Sedition Act of 1798.) Seditious libel, as such, disappeared from American law by the start of the nineteenth century; however, many later criminal libel actions were brought against citizens (or newspaper editors) who offended a judge, prosecutor, or some other local official.

Breach of the peace lasted longer. In an age when offended citizens were likely to take reprisals on their own (which in turn might set off family feuds that could last for generations), there was a societal interest in offering a legal alternative. Think, for a moment, about how frequently some insult on family honor was the cause of bloody battles and feuds in Shakespearean plays. The family name meant everything. That societal interest lessened as such bloody reprisals became less likely. Besides, the civil libel remedy was quicker, freighted with fewer philosophical problems, and—best of all—provided the offended person with what he could not get under criminal law: money. Sticks and stones may break your bones, but names can certainly hurt you; however, money will reduce the discomfort.

Legal scholars still debate whether the English law of criminal and seditious libel was transplanted to this country; no one doubts that the tort of libel was. There have always been fewer libel suits on this side of the Atlantic, and Chafee (1947) attributes this to the mobility of American society. An Englishman was rooted to his community and felt he had to vindicate a slur on his honor, whereas an American might either move on or avenge his honor with a pistol or horsewhip.

Today, libel is almost entirely a matter of civil law. It is exclusively a state matter; the federal government has no libel laws. As in any area of law, the Supreme Court polices the outer boundaries of state statutes and interpretations to make sure they are not grossly violative, but the court has repeatedly affirmed that state standards can vary and, in effect, has encouraged experimentation by the states.

The person who sues for libel must establish that the libel was published to at least one other person, that the publication damaged him or her, and that the person was identified in the libelous statement.

Since the essence of libel is loss of reputation, there can be no libel committed if a person calls another anything—unless it is read or overheard by a third party. No broadcast station or newspaper is likely to defend itself by saying nobody listens to or reads its product, but the question of publication sometimes arises in nonmedia cases.

Damages are another matter. Hurt feelings are not enough. The person bringing suit must show that he or she suffered in business affairs or in the esteem of friends or others in the community. What is damaging to one might not be to another. For example, a statement that a butcher was working on Friday night would not be libelous unless he was a kosher butcher catering to a Jewish trade. A husband would not normally be convicted of libel for suggesting that his wife had not been a virgin when they were married; however, in 1979 a Michigan man was convicted for saying that of his Sicilian wife, since in the Sicilian community that charge was taken quite seriously. (We will not concern ourselves with technical differences among the types of damages.)

Identification means that others could reasonably conclude that the person suing was the person referred to. If there are names, there are no questions about this, but some libels turn on veiled identifications or innuendo. Usually, it must be an individual who is identified, although sometimes a court will allow a small group to sue on the grounds that the libel hurt them all; however, it will not extend it to other, larger groups.

In most cases, one must prove falsity. Truth is an absolute defense in most states; in others, it is near-absolute. This is the reverse of the ancient legal shibboleth, "The greater the truth, the greater the libel." That logic was suggested by the fact that it was easier to refute obvious lies than truthful, but damaging, accusations; however, modern society has decided that a person should not be punished for publishing the truth, however unpleasant. Truth is the queen of defenses.

Many libel actions arise in the heat of a political or other campaign and are usually dropped quietly a few months later. But let us suppose Candidate A picks up the local daily paper and reads that Candidate B called him a Communist. Candidate A is outraged, but whom can he sue? Certainly he can sue Candidate B, and he undoubtedly will do so, for publicity purposes if for no other. But he can also sue the daily newspaper, the reporter, and its editors. Why? Because it is a hoary principle of libel that the tale bearer is as guilty as its originator. He can sue the newspaper and its personnel, even if what they published was a verbatim account of what Candidate B said in a meeting before thousands of people—or even if his words were carried by radio and television throughout the land. In that case, he may sue the broadcasters too, as tale bearers.

In modern defamation law, the media have little to worry about, assuming that what they published and broadcast was what Candidate B said. Courts seldom find the media guilty. First, they can plead truth, and second, they can plead privilege. The latter defense applies to fair and accurate accounts of public events of public concern, and especially of those tainted with official conduct.

The defenses of truth and qualified privilege are applicable to factual material; however, they are of little use in defending a libel suit based on opinion material. There is no way, for example, to prove the truth of a critic's opinion about a novel, a play, or a restaurant. In such cases, the defense rests on fair comment. Generally, the critic is in the clear if he keeps his comments focused on the work itself; only if he throws in gratuitous remarks about the personal lives of the authors or performers is he likely to find himself in serious libel difficulty.

The preceding remarks apply to all defamation actions, whether brought by public or private figures. Many state court decisions made it tougher for public figures to collect libel damages, even before the Supreme Court got around to its landmark 1964 decision, Times v. Sullivan (376 U.S. 254). Americans instinctively distrust politicians and insist on frequent elections and pitiless publicity for those in public positions. This strand runs through American history from the Revolutionary to the Jacksonian to the Progressive to the Watergate generations.

The Sullivan case was based on a full-page advertisement in the New York *Times* on behalf of individuals and groups protesting a "wave of terror" against blacks involved in nonviolent protests in the South. This in itself is significant, since up to that time the court had never clearly stated that material in ads was protected speech.

The plaintiff, a police commissioner, alleged that two paragraphs in the ad libeled him because it charged that the police, for whom he was responsible, had ringed the Alabama State College campus with shotguns and tear gas and had used trumped up charges to arrest peaceful demonstrators. In the course of the libel trial, those who placed the ad admitted that it contained several factual errors. The Alabama jury found the ministers and the *Times* guilty and assessed a fine of $500,000.

Justice William Brennan in the Supreme Court opinion insisted that the case be considered "against the background of a profound national commitment to the principle that debate on public issues should be uninhibited, robust, and wide-open, and that it may well include vehement, caustic, and sometimes unpleasantly sharp attacks on government and public officials." Erroneous statements did not automatically disqualify a work or ad from First Amendment protection. The core paragraph of his opinion reads:

The constitutional guarantees require, we think, a federal rule that prohibits a public official from recovering damages for a defamatory falsehood relating to his official conduct unless he proves that the statement was made with "actual malice"—that is, with knowledge that it was false or with reckless disregard of whether it was false or not.

Brennan then pointed out that such a privilege was analogous to the protection accorded public officials when they were sued by private individuals. The court had held such utterances, made in the line of public duty, immune from libel actions.

The court found no actual malice in the publication of the ad, and in reversing the decision set libel on its modern course. Subsequent opinions applied the Sullivan malice standard to elected and appointed officials and to candidates for public office. Then came public figures, those who voluntarily thrust themselves into public controversies.

In 1971 a plurality of the Supreme Court in Rosenbloom v. Metromedia (403 U.S. 29) took the trend to its extreme. In reporting a police obscenity raid on a magazine distributor, a local television station made some false and defamatory statements about the distributor who, after being acquitted on the obscenity charge, sued the station. Was the distributor a public figure for libel purposes? He certainly had not wanted to be in the spotlight, but the court said that he was, whether he wanted to be or not. It was the nature of the event, not his personal notoriety, that granted the media wide discretion in coverage. The standard of actual malice applied. Although several states adopted the Rosenbloom logic of newsworthy events, the Supreme Court soon abandoned it, finding a prominent society woman who held press conferences throughout her lengthy and highly publicized divorce case and a man who had once been convicted of an infamous crime both private figures.

In Gertz v. Welch (418 U. S. 323) in 1974, the Court held that a nationally prominent criminal lawyer was not a public figure. Although he was well-known in legal circles, few others knew his name. He had been called a "Communist-fronter" and several other names by a conservative magazine for agreeing to prosecute, on behalf of the family of a slain boy, the policeman who had done the shooting. The court said that states could set lesser standards of proof for those ruled private figures. That lesser standard is negligence. Some states adopted this policy, but others retained the Rosenbloom "issue" logic.

There will probably never be a precise definition of a public figure. Some trial courts have included teachers, coaches, and local entertainers, while others have found just the opposite. In 1979 the Supreme Court declared that a research scientist was not a public figure, although he had a $500,000 grant from a federal agency. A senator had made fun of his project, and the scientist sued. The court said the scientist did not have access to the media to refute the senator's jibes. The more access the person has to the media, the more chance he has to refute charges hurled at him. It is a sort of free marketplace of ideas rationale: Make sure all points of view are expressed and let the public decide.

For those declared public figures, there was little prospect of winning libel cases until 1979, when in Herbert v. Lando (441 U.S. 153), the Supreme Court ruled they had a right to inquire into the motives and attitudes of reporters and editors. The court saw it as a logical extension of the Sullivan rationale. How else could a public figure show that material had been published with reckless disregard as to whether it was true or not? The press overreacted to this decision more than to any other in years, painting it as an invitation for attorneys to pry into the minds of reporters; however, there was no apparent upsurge in the numbers of public figures suing or winning libel cases in its wake.

Libel actions are relatively rare today. An attorney for a large metropolitan daily reports that about 30 to 40 suits are filed each year against his paper, and that only one or two of these go as far as pretrial discovery. Another said that in 20 years, he had been to court ten times. In the first 40 years of *Time*, Inc., 325 libel cases were filed, of which twelve were paid off and a total of nine lost at trial. When cases go to trial, juries find about half the time for media defendants and about half the time for plaintiffs; however, some convictions are reversed by appellate courts.

From a societal point of view, it is not important whether a defendant collects dollars for what has been published or broadcast about him. In civil actions of all kinds, the state is impartial, providing only the courtroom, rules, and procedures for airing the dispute. So long as the trial is conducted within the broad range of reasonableness, the government has no special interest. If something about it is grossly unfair, then it is violative of the equal protection under the law ideal and becomes a matter to be reviewed.

Jury awards in libel cases have become astronomical. The court had been alarmed in 1964 about the $500,000 award in Sullivan; in 1981 there was an award of $26.5 million. That award, like many others, was later reduced by the appellate courts, but libel decisions of $1 million or more have become commonplace. The implications of such monetary penalties for the smalltime publisher or speaker are obvious.

It is different in other countries. For example, in Great Britain there is a tradition of the one-cent settlement. That means that a court can find for the plaintiff and clear his name without insisting on monetary recompense. It is vital to remember, however, that under the British system the loser bears all the legal and court costs, whereas in the United States each side pays its own attorneys. In France there are frequent libel suits, but the maximum recovery is the equivalent of $2500. French courts can order the convicted paper to publish a retraction and even to purchase advertising space in other publications to print the retractions. There are no similar powers in American courts.

Emerson (1970) concluded that libel laws do more good than harm for a society. If nothing else, they make the mass media more cautious. He admitted that was a mixed blessing, since controversies need airing, not covering up. All in all, he found that libel laws have had a remarkably minor impact on the system of free expression, mostly because libel litigation is slow, costly, and complex and juries wildly unpredictable in their findings.

Those who would interpret the First Amendment in absolutist terms ("Congress shall make no law. . .") find all libel laws unconstitutional. Justice Hugo Black was the only justice to take that position, arguing that if society wanted to protect reputations, it would have to amend the First Amendment. Other jurists are willing to accept the encroachment because they think protecting reputations is more important. As with obscenity, the debate turns on where the line is drawn. All speech outside that line (obscenity, libel, treason, fighting words) lacks First Amendment protection.

# 8

## NEWER TECHNOLOGIES THAT SHAPED THE FIRST AMENDMENT

**Both photography and broadcasting have been regulated because of their intrusive nature. Broadcast licensing has rested on the shortage of airwaves, but new technology threatens that traditional logic.**

The print media enjoy their special legal protections, in part because they have been around longer than the other media and in part because they are considered more serious and more dignified. Most historical arguments for free expression have been made on behalf of the print media. At least since the time of John Milton, Western philosophers have framed their arguments for free expression in terms of serious people discussing serious matters. Only gradually have those arguments been extended to entertainment content, and in their earliest periods the new media of still photography, motion picture photography, and broadcasting were primarily, if not exclusively, concerned with entertaining, rather than informing or persuading, audiences.

It was only in the closing decades of the nineteenth century that newspapers and magazines made extensive use of photographs. Respectable people cursed them—as they did the flamboyant make-up, the screaming headlines, and the gutter stories—as "yellow journalism." In many ways, photographs were the worst, since brash photographers intruded to get their pictures, and then the media printed them without so much as an artist's assistance in "prettying them up." Certainly, governmental bodies, and especially courts, did not want photographers spoiling the decorum of their sessions (Lofton, 1966).

Broadcasters have faced even more regulatory discrimination. Broadcasting's regulation rests on its use of a scarce public resource, the airwaves. If a person wants to publish his own book, magazine, or newspaper, he does not have to get permission from anyone; however, the person who wants to broadcast must first attain a license from the federal government. This has been justified on the grounds that more persons want to broadcast than the spectrum can accommodate; therefore, the government must choose. In the 1980s it was clear that emerging technologies—cable, satellite, direct-to-home, laser, and others—were eroding that rationale.

In this chapter we will consider privacy law, the question of cameras in the courtrooms and, finally, the special status of broadcast regulation.

## CAMERAS, MICROPHONES, AND PRIVACY

Most people agree that there is, or ought to be, some zone of privacy into which a person may retreat and expect to be left alone. Although some speak of this as a natural right, there was little experience with or legal recognition of it before this century. The demands have been fueled by the increasingly sophisticated and miniaturized gadgets of surveillance (such as wiretaps, parabolic microphones, concealed recorders, and cameras that operate in the dark).

Miller (1971) did not discount these devices but insisted that the burgeoning system of collecting, storing, and retrieving data posed even greater threats to modern privacy. Credit agencies, schools, employers, and governmental units all compile electronic records, as do the military and police. In spite of legal attempts to regulate these systems, the data banks grow and are shared more and more.

The tort of privacy is narrower, and it is with this area of civil law that we will deal. Probably no area of law was so shaped by a law journal article as was privacy. Samuel Warren and Louis Brandeis (1890) argued in the *Harvard Law Review* that a law of privacy could be pieced together from strands of property law and awards for mental anguish. Others had suggested this before, but their article excited interest in the topic.

Brandeis (who four decades later would be a distinguished Supreme Court justice) apparently wrote most of the article. The immediate spur supposedly was the bad manners shown by the Boston newspapers in covering the events surrounding the marriage of Warren's daughter. Pember (1972), however, found the Boston papers of the day fairly staid, and while they carried some gossip, there was almost no sexual innuendo.

But there was one important ingredient that had just been added to daily newspaper journalism: action photography. Photos, by their nature, are intrusive. Many people do not like to have their pictures taken, and in some parts of the world it is a serious breach of morals to take someone's photograph. Adding to the intrusiveness of the photographers of the 1890s was the nature of their equipment. It was big and bulky, and the flash apparatus was noisy, smoky, and a nuisance to everyone in the same room.

Some of the accusations against the press of the late nineteenth century sounded much like this comment, taken from a letter between two noblemen of ancient Rome. Twenty centuries before Warren and Brandeis, they were complaining about the commercial (handwritten) newsletters of their day:

> The press is overstepping . . . the obvious bounds of propriety and decency. Gossip . . . has become a trade. . . . The details of sexual relations are spread broadcast. . . . Column upon column is filled with idle gossip.

Warren and Brandeis clearly exaggerated, but they were applauded by the legal community, among whose number have always been many press critics.

Anglo-American law was slow to develop an interest in protecting strictly personal rights. When it did so, it usually did its best to phrase the rulings in terms of property rights. It is easier to demonstrate damage and to set recompense for infractions of property rights, after all. Great Britain, in fact, has never developed a tort of privacy.

If Warren and Brandeis were upset primarily by what the news media were publishing, it is somewhat ironic that the first privacy cases were not media-related. The first notorious case involved a flour company that had reprinted a picture of an attractive young lady on advertising posters without her permission. She collected $15,000 in New York at the trial level but had the decision overturned because there was no law of privacy. That decision so outraged the New York legislature that it enacted a privacy law in 1903 making it illegal to use the name, portrait, or picture of anyone for advertising or "trade purposes" without that person's consent. It was a narrow law, based on property rights, and it was copied as other states got into the area. Even so, it was not exactly a rush. In the next 20 years, Pember points out, four more states enacted laws and five recognized a common law protection for privacy. By 1980, all but a few states had either enacted a privacy law or had recognized some form of common law of privacy.

Again, it is worth noting that this first major case turned on a photographic image, as have a large percentage of the cases since. A 1909 New York case was brought against the producer of a newsreel who recreated a steamship collision. The film depicted the way a real-life wireless operator had stayed heroically at his post and had been responsible for saving many lives. The operator did not like his name and (dramatized) actions being shown and sued. The New York court said his image had been exploited by the film company for its own profit (Binns v. Vitagraph, 103 N.E. 1108, 1913). By then courts had ruled that newspapers and magazines, even though they were published for profit, could publish such descriptions and photos. The print media had First Amendment protection, whereas the infant movie industry did not.

With the development of instant photography came another case, but again it had no direct media connection. The owner of a bar in rural Wisconsin apparently entertained his customers by taking photos of ladies using his rest room. One of the ladies was outraged enough to sue at common law, arguing that if that was not an invasion of privacy, what was? The state supreme court sympathized, but said that since the legislature had not seen fit to enact a protection for privacy, it had no power to find one. (The Wisconsin legislature soon enacted one.)

In the 1970s, Jacqueline Kennedy Onassis had a running feud with a photographer who trailed her and her children around. They had some physical as well as legal run-ins. She sued for a variety of wrongs, including invasion of privacy, but eventually withdrew all monetary claims in return for injunctive relief. The judge ordered the photographer to keep his distance and finally to take no more pictures at all of her or her children. Another photographer published what purported, at least, to be photos taken of the former First Lady sunbathing in the nude, aboard a yacht, far at sea.

An interesting privacy case, turning on appropriation, was settled by the Supreme Court in 1977. A "human cannonball" collected from a local television station for filming his "entire act" and showing it on the evening news without his consent. He made no claim that the showing had interfered with his popularity or decreased his income, but only that he had the right to decide how to capitalize on his act (Zacchini v. Scripps-Howard, 433 U.S. 562,

1977). In short, there is an implicit "right to publicity" that is of concern to those in public life. The vast majority of privacy cases concern those in acting, entertainment, sports, or other aspects of public life.

Usually, a photographer or a television cameraman can film anything accessible to the public view; it is only when he starts filming more intimate settings that he runs into difficulty. Also, the manner of intrusion can be a factor. Courts held it an invasion of privacy when a TV crew burst into a fancy New York restaurant and began filming the diners. It wanted to illustrate a news story, saying that the posh eatery had been cited that week for sanitary violations. Although the restaurant was a public place, the filming, over the protests of the manager, created chaos (some diners reportedly dived under tables) and constituted an invasion of privacy.

Photographers, television or still, must be careful about taking photos in private places. For example, a Kansas City woman won a privacy action against Time, Inc., for publishing a picture taken of her in a hospital where she was being treated for a rare disease that caused her to eat almost constantly but still lose weight. *Time* published it under the caption "Starving Glutton."

A Florida newspaper photographer was sued for invasion of privacy after trying to lend a hand to a fire marshal. The marshal asked him to take a photo of the silhouette of a victim left on the floor of a burned home. The photo went into the official files, but also into the newspaper. The mother of the victim said the photographer had no business there, but the court dismissed the claim, finding it common practice for photographers to accompany fire investigators.

Both cameras and microphones were involved in a decision that upheld a privacy award to a medical quack. A magazine was preparing a story on medical quackery and heard about a Los Angeles practitioner. Two staff members posed as a husband and wife, made an appointment, and saw the doctor. They had arranged with police in advance to carry microphones, so the police could hear and record what transpired. The doctor used some gadgets and announced that the female reporter's health problems could be traced to some rancid butter she had eaten exactly 11 years, 9 months, and 7 days earlier. They left, and then with photographers covered the arrest of the doctor. The court had great troubles with the case, admitting that the reporters helped rid society of a faker, but at the same time being offended by their subterfuge (Dietemann v. Time, 449 F.2d. 245, 1971).

Warren and Brandeis, in their famous article, conceded, "The right to privacy ceases upon the publication of the facts by the individual or with his consent." Consent can be tricky, however, as these two cases illustrate.

A black girl was sitting on the steps of her high school one day when a professional photographer came up, introduced himself, and asked if she would mind posing for a picture. She agreed and thought nothing more about it until about a year later when she found that picture illustrating a section of a book on the special problems of minorities in getting into college. She claimed she was embarrassed and sued for privacy damages, although in the trial she admitted that almost none of her friends had seen the picture until she showed it to them. She won her case.

In a much more famous case, a macho surfer talked freely with a magazine reporter. He also posed for pictures on the beach. When he found out the article included his quotations about his bizarre lifestyle, he objected that he had consented to be quoted only about his favorite sport. It took nearly a decade and untold legal fees before the magazine won that privacy case (Virgil v. Time, Inc., 527 F.2d. 1122, 1975).

Privacy, like any tort action, normally dies with the individual. The heirs of Bela Lugosi and Laurel and Hardy lost their claims to some of the payments made to movie companies for the right to reproduce pictures of the late celebrities on teeshirts and other products. The courts said that these men had not established their movie images or *persona* during their own lifetime, and hence they could not be claimed by their heirs. One star who did, and whose heirs have collected, was W. C. Fields. During his lifetime, he blazed trails in finding ways to promote himself on posters and products. The U.S. Postal Service was shocked in 1980 when it decided to issue a commemorative stamp with Fields's picture and had to make a token payment to his heirs. Even in this series of cases, which clearly lie on the fringe, the debate is over the use of the photographic image, not words.

## CAMERAS IN THE COURTROOM

Both by tradition and law, a judge has almost total discretion in setting the rules for those who appear in his courtroom, either as participants or as spectators. Appellate courts rarely second-guess him in these matters.

Most judges will do all they can to isolate the proceedings from outside contamination. For example, they may postpone trials until public interest flags, or during trials they may sequester juries. It is not surprising that they look askance at media coverage. Most of them have learned, with reluctance, to live with newspaper reporters, but even that was not easy. Well into the present century, judges who did not like the way a newspaper was covering a trial would often slap it or its reporter with a contempt citation. This type of out-of-court contempt is called constructive contempt and has all but disappeared today. The Supreme Court dealt it a near-fatal blow in 1941 (Bridges v. California, 314 U.S. 252).

At the same time, there has been a long series of decisions holding that the constitutional right to a public trial does not require that the judge allow newsmen to be present. It is a right of the accused and can be satisfied, usually, if some of his family or advisors are present during the portions closed to the public.

If newspaper reporters with their pencils and pads are a possible distraction, then reporters employing more obstructive equipment are even more so. Most judges steadfastly refused requests by still photographers, newsreel photographers, and radio broadcasters to cover important trials; however for many years, the judge could grant such privileges if he chose. Some of the most sensational cases of the 1920s were conducted with photographers present. These included the 1924 trial of Loeb and Leopold for the murder of Bobby Franks in Chicago and the 1925 Scopes evolution trial in Dayton, Tennessee. In the latter, the judge permitted live radio coverage.

Few trials in American history have received wider attention than that of Bruno Hauptmann in 1935. He was accused of the kidnap and murder of the baby of Charles and Ann Morrow Lindbergh. More than 700 reporters and 130 photographers crowded the little burgh of Flemington, New Jersey. The milling crowds of the curious were estimated at 20,000 in a single day. The small courtroom was turned into a 24-hour news distributing center from which thousands of words flowed every day. Both the prosecution and the defense attorneys leaked information shamelessly to the press, in hopes of improving their chances for victory in the trial. Papers throughout the country emblazoned the accounts with inflammatory headlines. Editorials called Hauptmann a thug, an inhuman beast, and worse. He was convicted, but the carnival atmosphere of the trial was to have far more lasting effects (Gillmor, 1966).

In 1937, the American Bar Association adopted a canon against allowing cameras or broadcast equipment in courtrooms. The federal bar enacted this canon into a rule, as did the majority of states. In 1952, the ABA added television to the ban.

Most of the early opposition was couched in terms of the intrusive equipment, requiring as it did artificial lighting and highly visible gear. Technology slowly corrected these problems, but the ABA refused to reverse itself, insisting that a televised trial was inherently unfair. The Supreme Court upheld that contention in 1965 (Estes v. Texas, 38 U.S. 532).

In the mid-1970s, some states looked at the question again. Clearly, there had been major advances in the technology that permitted both still and television photography with natural light and with miniaturized equipment. The ABA even conceded this, but the technological advances did not remove their fears that the presence of cameras would interfere with justice in other, more subtle ways. Would the trial participants be made nervous? Would they tailor their reactions for the cameras? Would jurors be subjected to more pressures outside the courtrooms? Would witnesses and jurors be afraid to testify? There was little scientific research evidence to answer these questions.

Florida was among the states that took the lead in experimenting in 1977. The rules were drawn carefully, and the presiding judges given great discretion in minimizing the physical intrusion of the cameras. Most jurors said they quickly forgot about the one camera and one crewmen operating from a fixed and unobtrusive position. Coverage was pooled, with TV stations making videotape recordings in a separate room. The judge could order the camera shut off during any particularly sensitive testimony. Even critics of the experiments agreed that broadcasting was no longer a threat to the decorum of trials, but that did not answer the other objections, particularly in the case of the Florida rules that differed from most states in that they permitted a judge to allow televising *even over the objection of the accused.* (Most other states allowed the accused to veto such coverage.)

It was in Florida that the test case arose. Two Miami Beach policemen were accused of committing a burglary, and while the case had some bizarre aspects (e.g., an insomniac heard them on his

CB radio, conversing while carrying out the theft in the wee hours of the morning), it was strictly of local interest. The policemen objected to the TV cameras, but the judge permitted them, and the local station carried less than three minutes on an evening newscast. Convicted, the policemen appealed to the Supreme Court, claiming that the Estes decision had meant that cameras, by their mere presence, prevented a fair and unbiased trial. In 1981 the Supreme Court, in Chandler v. Florida (449 U.S. 560), sidestepped that issue, deciding instead that states had the right to experiment with cameras in the courtroom.

At the time of the decision, more than half the states had some provision for televising certain types of judicial proceedings, and while the court did not rule on the First Amendment aspects, the Chandler decision clearly encouraged states to be flexible. No one thought that the issue was closed; in fact, the decision merely opened it further.

## REGULATION OF AIRWAVES

Radio or television broadcasters use a limited and valuable natural resource: space on the electromagnetic spectrum. That makes their regulation fundamentally different from the print media. Most governments keep the broadcast spectrum for themselves. The overwhelming number of systems in the world are government-owned and operated.

The United States chose another pattern. It decided to allocate most of the broadcast spectrum to private licensees; however, the government retained the right to decide who got the licenses and to review periodically the performance of the licensees. A government commission was to make sure they broadcast in the public interest.

When radio telegraphy emerged at the turn of the century, it found its principal use to be as a maritime aid. It simplified and speeded messages between ships and between ships and shore points. As early as 1903 there were international conferences urging that all ships be fitted with the apparatus, and the United States enacted such a law in 1910. It was the first American law dealing with radio. The law was strengthened in 1912 following the disastrous sinking of the luxury liner *Titanic*. The ship nearest the disaster had equipment but only one operator, and he was asleep when the distress signal came.

Radio telegraphy, like the telegraph and the telephone, was fundamentally a point-to-point communication, more akin to interpersonal communication than to mass. There were experiments throughout the world in the early years of this century that would result in the emergence of radio broadcasting as a mass medium. Some focused on dots and dashes, but others transmitted the human voice and music. These developments came to a halt in 1917 when the federal government seized radio and put it to work in the war effort. With the end of the war, radio was set for a boom that even its stoutest champions could not have predicted (Head and Sterling, 1982).

Amateurs had been sending messages for a long time, but in 1920 there emerged serious stations broadcasting on a regular basis. Everyone seemed to be building a crystal set to hear the words and music from such distant cities as Pittsburgh and Detroit. Of the nearly 600 stations on the air in mid-1923, nearly 40 percent were owned by radio and electrical manufacturers and dealers. Another one-fourth were divided almost equally between schools and newspapers, and the remainder (many of them shoestring operations that would soon throw in the towel) between a dismaying variety of commercial and noncommercial groups. By 1922, stores were selling ready-made sets. They sold more than 4 million of them by 1929.

There were no commercials at first, but by 1923 they were creeping in. By 1925, it was clear that America's broadcasting system—unlike that in most of the rest of the world—would be financed by advertising. The establishment of radio networks, which could afford to bring the most popular entertainment by pooling both the costs and the advertising profits among participating stations, set that pattern indelibly.

In less than a decade, radio moved from an experiment to a household necessity, and those who operated the stations, owned the key patents, leased the lines, and manufactured the sets profited accordingly. All of this went on with almost no government supervision. As Rosen (1980) makes clear, the scramble for control of broadcasting went on at many levels during the formative years before Congress set the pattern with the comprehensive Radio Act of 1927. That act, as amended in 1934, remains the fundamental regulation for not only radio but for television and the myriad new technologies that have arisen since. The system that emerged in 1927 was a result of the interplay among businessmen, the prospective market, politics, and bureaucrats. The navy, and to a lesser degree the army, wanted to keep the system for their own use, but so did the multiplying hordes of amateur wireless operators. Existing institutions could not supervise radio. Into that vacuum the Department of Commerce stepped and asserted control. Commerce employees staffed and set the agenda for the series of national radio conferences that preceded the congressional act that established the Federal Radio Commission, and the new agency was staffed by former commerce experts. "Commerce," of course, meant not only the cabinet-level agency of that name but also "commerce" (with a lower case c), because it evolved in such a way as to be most useful to businessmen. It is not coincidental that 1927 was the year after the first network emerged, a network whose costly programs were sure to be supported by advertising.

In truth, radio was a victim of its own success. Stations crowded one another, overlapped signals, and generally created chaos. There would have to be decisions about how to divide the spectrum among those who wanted to use it.

The 1927 Federal Radio Act created a commission charged with providing "fair, efficient, and equitable radio service" to all areas of the country. It was to decide among competing applicants on the basis of "public interest, convenience and necessity." In 1933, only two years after the Supreme Court told Minnesota it could not ban Jacob Near's newspaper because of what he had published earlier (see Chapter 5, this volume), it upheld a circuit court's decision that the FRC could refuse to relicense a radio station to a California minister on almost exactly the same grounds. The minister had used the station to attack government officials, labor groups, and other religions; Near had aimed his printed barbs at those same targets.

In Trinity Methodist Church, South v. FRC (62 F.2d. 850), the circuit court had written:

This is neither censorship nor previous restraint, nor is it a whittling away of the rights guaranteed by the First Amendment, or an impairment of their free exercise. Appellant may continue to indulge his strictures upon the characters of men in public office. He may just as freely as ever criticize religious practices of which he does not approve. He may even indulge private malice or personal slander—subject, of course, to being required to answer for the abuse thereof—but he may not, as we think, demand, of right, the continued use of an instrumentality of commerce for such purposes, or any other, except in subordination to all reasonable rules and regulations Congress, acting through the Commission, may prescribe.

The law insists that radio is not to be treated like a public utility. Operators of a public utility such as a bus line or an electrical company are required to serve all applicants on a first-come, first-served basis. They may not use discrimination in selecting their customers. Those assigned a broadcasting license, on the other hand, are told to discriminate. They are to decide what is aired over their respective stations, and they alone are responsible for everything that is broadcast there. They cannot escape responsibility by saying the program came from the network or that the advertisement came from an agency. If it goes out over the station, they are responsible.

From the beginning, the federal agency (renamed the Federal Communications Commission in the 1934 law) required reports on what a station was broadcasting. The FCC cannot order a station not to carry a particular program, although it may advise caution. It can take into account the overall pattern of programming during the preceding license period when deciding whether to renew. In fact, though, it almost never takes away a license because of programming. It is more likely to do so for technical violations, such as not staying on the assigned frequency. The FCC can also reprimand a station, as it did after the Carlin broadcast (see Chapter 6, this volume).

It also limits the number of stations an individual or a corporation can own. Today, the limit is seven TV stations (no more than five of them VHF), seven AM, and seven FM radio stations. There are also limits on regional concentration. Diversity of both ownership and content has been a consistent major policy goal. Networks make something of a mockery of this, since under law they are considered pooling arrangements among individual stations and therefore not licensed. They are, however, licensed as owners of their own stations. Since surveys show that during prime time hours, 90 percent of the TV sets are tuned to either ABC, CBS, or NBC (the remainder scattered among public stations, syndicated shows, or local programs), the networks do dominate American viewing habits, just as the radio networks once dominated listening. Radio became essentially a local medium when television robbed it of its mass audiences and its national advertisers in about 1950.

As we have seen, philosophers, lawmakers, and courts have been most protective of the print media's right to express opinions on issues of public concern. They have been much more willing to protect that than the right to entertain, for example. It is ironic, therefore, to find that the priorities are reversed with broadcast regulation. The rules limit opinion matter more than any other kind.

Given the shortage of spectrum rationale, it is understandable that the federal government pays careful attention to what a licensee says about public controversies, both in news and special events and in broadcast editorials. No station owner should be allowed to use the public franchise to espouse only one point of view.

News broadcasts were not a regular part of early broadcasting, although there were frequent bulletins. Apparently no one even thought of broadcasting editorials until the late 1930s. The FCC decided that was a bad idea and issued a ban on all editorials in 1941. The best indication of how little interest there was among broadcasters is that there was almost no outcry or complaint. Most broadcasters knew they were in the entertainment business, and there were far higher profits to be made there than in editorials, which by their nature were certain to make some people angry.

The FCC lifted the ban in 1949, replacing it with the Fairness Doctrine. Each station could now cover and comment on controversies; however, it had to provide adequate opportunity for opposing viewpoints. It sounded simple enough.

It was 1969 (Red Lion v. FCC 395 U.S. 367) before the Supreme Court ruled on the constitutionality of the Fairness Doctrine, and it upheld the doctrine by a unanimous vote. In another case, decided the same day, the court also upheld a closely related FCC rule that required a station airing a personal attack on an individual to notify the target individual and invite him to reply.

Broadcasters argued that the fear of triggering these Fairness Doctrine mechanisms, with their attendant demands on time and money, actually silenced controversy. They argued that this self-imposed censorship reduced, rather than enhanced, the free and open discussion of public issues. The court rejected this argument and insisted:

> It does not violate the First Amendment to treat licensees given the privilege of using scarce radio frequencies as proxies for the entire community, obligated to give suitable time and attention to matters of great public concern. To condition the granting of renewal of licenses on a willingness to present representative community views on controversial issues is consistent with the ends and purposes of those constitutional provisions forbidding the abridgement of freedom of speech and freedom of the press.

Many constitutional scholars found it strange that the court did not even refer to its Red Lion decision five years later in its Miami Herald v. Tornillo (418 U.S. 241) decision. In that case, the court told Florida it could not require the print media to grant a right of reply to a political candidate who had been assailed by a rival in that same paper.

In recent years, the scope of the Fairness Doctrine has been shrunk. For example, it does not apply to commercial messages or to controversies that are not of general public concern.

Section 315 of the Federal Communications Act requires that during election periods stations treat in an equitable manner bona fide candidates for the same office. Appearances on news programs are excluded. Although there are difficulties in deciding when a campaign is on (in this era when candidates, especially for the White House, never stop running), and in defining a candidate, this section creates far fewer problems than does the Fairness Doctrine. It has forced fancy footwork on the part of networks to stage debates among the two or three major party candidates for president without having to provide equal time for every splinter party candidate. The goals of Section 315 and the Fairness Doctrine are the same, namely to encourage the airing of ideas and views. A crabbed interpretation of either that would deprive the electorate of their opportunity to see the major party candidates in a head-to-head confrontation certainly would not further that goal.

Citizens do write to the FCC. Most of the 70,000 complaints received in 1979-80 were couched in general complaints about particular programs or series, often that they were too violent or too sexy. Relatively few raise specific fairness or 315 charges (Head and Sterling, 1982).

Many responsible critics insist that the FCC's pretenses at regulation have been frauds. Certainly, the commission has been no more than a reluctant dragon, and in the 1980s the mood of deregulation has put out even that fire. In the 35 years up to 1978, it revoked 40 and refused to renew another 98 licenses, mostly for boondock radio stations with appalling histories of complaints and noncompliance. Most of the revocations and nonrenewals were for technical or ownership reasons, not for content.

In 1981 Congress extended the duration of radio licenses from three to seven years, and of television licenses from three to five years, thus reducing the number of times citizens groups could exert pressure on them to improve hiring practices or program content.

## NEWER DELIVERY SYSTEMS

Policymakers have looked around in the 1980s and realized that new delivery systems—cable, direct broadcasts from satellites, relays, low power stations, videodiscs, videocassettes, and others still on the drawing board—promise a television of abundance, not of shortage. Still, all the regulatory rationale has been based on shortage. Clearly, there will have to be major rethinking of these problems.

In keeping with the deregulatory mood, there are those who urge the abandonment of content regulations on over-the-air broadcasters so that they could compete on an even basis with the new systems. Others have cautioned that most of the new systems were still not a reality for many homes, so that even if deregulation were the right answer, the time is not yet ripe for it.

Videotex and teletext systems, because they provide words instead of pictures, pose additional regulatory problems. Many of these systems are services and operated by local newspaper owners, and much of their content is identical to that which appears in printed media. Should the words on the cathode ray tube be regulated as broadcast or as print? The FCC decided in 1982 that they were not subject to fairness or 315 rules, but that left broader policy questions unanswered.

Cable television has the longest history, tracing its ancestry back to 1950 when residents of small towns in valleys built community antennae up on the hills in order to bring in the signals from distant cities. Each subscriber's set was hooked to the master antenna by a cable and the owners paid a small monthly fee for the privilege. It was not long before some system operators began to generate limited local programming—perhaps covering the school board meetings or local basketball games—in order to attract even more subscribers. Some then started renting feature films and showing them to cable subscribers.

The FCC was early in asserting its jurisdiction over cable television, and after two decades of litigation, the courts had generally upheld this power; however, in the meantime, cable had expanded drastically. Operators added pay services, brought in distant cities, and subscribed for added programming either from superstations that bounced their signals off satellites or with program services designed the same way. Inevitably, the local owners sold to chain owners. By 1980, over-the-air broadcasters owned one-third of American cable systems, and publishers of newspapers and magazines owned another one-fourth. Many of the others were in the hands of multiple-system (chain) operators (Head and Sterling, 1982). It was also clear that effective regulatory power had shifted to local communities, most of which awarded an exclusive franchise to an operator and then held the firm responsible for what it aired. This was a major change from over-the-air broadcasting, which was the exclusive regulatory domain of the federal, not state and local, government. It should be noted that cable television does not use up space on the spectrum; its programming comes in by wire or satellite beam and is distributed on wires to subscriber homes.

There was a steady spread of cable systems in the quarter-century from 1955 to 1980. The number of systems grew from 400 to nearly 5,000 and the number of subscribers from 150,000 to nearly 20 million. Many of the systems could carry a dozen or more channels. Most people admitted that they subscribed more to get a good picture than for diversity in programming, but for whatever reason they signed up, about 30 percent of American homes were wired by the end of 1981. Cabling went faster in rural than urban areas, not only because of the higher demand for a clear picture, but because the political problems of awarding franchises were much simpler. The same promised to be true of low-power television, approved by the FCC in 1982.

In Home Box Office v. FCC (567 F.2d. 9, 1977), the court chastised the FCC for being unduly protectionist with regard to existing over-the-air broadcasters. While the decision dealt specifically with pay-TV rules, it forced the commission to reconsider its whole cable policy. By 1980, the FCC had announced that it now sought to encourage competition between cable and regular broadcasters, and to that end it was dropping its rules limiting the channels that systems could and could not carry, as well as its requirement that cable systems provide access channels for locals desiring to air a program or message. It even eliminated the requirement that a cable system obtain approval from the FCC to go into business or to sell to someone else.

Canada's experience with cable television has been quite different. In the early 1970s the Ottawa government made an enormous commitment of resources, promising to bring cable or satellite delivery of television pictures to every household in that vast, sprawling land. It made considerable progress toward that goal (Canada is one of the most heavily cabled nations in the world) but ran into rising regionalism. The provinces, both those in the West and in French-speaking Quebec, resisted the inroads from the federal government. They asserted the right to control at least part of the content aired within their borders. Problems of a different sort came when operators of cable systems in cities along the American border began offering the American programs at the expense of Canadian content. That raised issues both economic and cultural.

Distribution systems are frightfully expensive, of course. Even satellite systems, considerably cheaper than those tied to cables and telephone lines, involve tremendous start-up costs. How a nation deals with this problem depends largely on geography and the size of its population. Canada, for example, with one-tenth the population of the United States scattered across a land mass that reaches 3500 miles, invests most of its communication resources in transmission systems. A compact nation like Great Britain invests in programming. Australia realized as it became a major producer of quality movies and television series that it must rely on the export trade; the Australian market was too small to support the heavy investments. The problems are even more acute for non-English speaking nations, because they have more difficulty finding markets abroad. Japan, for example, can sell relatively little programming abroad, and since it is a fairly compact nation, it can invest in distribution systems. Indeed, it has some of the most advanced distribution systems in the world and led in the development of high-definition television, which with many more dots to the inch could present far clearer pictures than older systems. The Japanese have also led the world in experiments with facsimile delivery of information. That means printing out information in "hard copy" right at the home or office set receiver.

In 1980, Ted Turner of Atlanta started an all-news television service to which cable system operators could subscribe at a nominal monthly rate and that they could then deliver to their own subscribers as an incentive, something over-the-air stations did not have. Officials of the established networks scoffed at the upstart Cable News Network, which operated initially with a skeleton staff and a minuscule budget. However, within two years one of the networks was discussing a possible merger with Turner. Much of the content tended to be headlines, repeated more frequently, but there were also features and a few in-depth reports. During the Polish crisis of 1982, for example, the network often carried long segments that were being shown on Polish television, with voice-over explanations. The regular networks were not likely to devote their time to such material. CNN put together a five-part series on brain cancer among chemical workers in the Texas Gulf region and had the time to run it. It also devoted long hours to unspectacular events such as congressional hearings.

If, on the whole, the offerings of CNN were not drastically different from those on commercial network news, that is not surprising, since nearly all the personnel were trained in the commercial medium. James Traub (1981) concluded: "Anything that dents the networks' monopoly of national news must be considered good; but anything that does so essentially by adopting the networks' own standards ultimately gives little cause for rejoicing."

Turner also owns WTBS, the "superstation" that sends its programs to cable systems around the country via satellite. Much of that programming consists of Atlanta Braves and Atlanta Hawks games. Not incidentally, Turner owns both ball clubs.

The three broadcasting networks, accustomed to dividing up 90 to 95 percent of the prime-time audience among themselves, began to take notice of cable in the late 1970s because in areas where a large proportion of homes were hooked to cable, they were dividing up only 70 to 75 percent. The networks were into their own plans for cable systems.

With increased viewers came the first significant trickle of advertising dollars. During 1981, the cable industry's advertising income doubled from the year before, and by 1990 was expected to be $2.5 billion. Cable presented a challenge to agencies to design new advertising formats. A likely model was Music Television, a 24-hour rock music channel, which began in 1981. The producers sell and insert six minutes of advertising each hour (mostly to record companies whose songs and stars the channel promotes) and then offer the program, via satellite, to local cable system operators. They even leave a two-minute space each hour that can be sold locally. The systems pay almost nothing for the programming, offering it on one of their channels, and thus giving another incentive to subscribe. Similar channels were being developed for foods, health products, and others that might be attractive to advertisers. More and more, these elements of cable television were looking like magazines.

Cable television is changing at a dizzying pace, and still more radical distribution systems are on the horizon, many of them tied in one way or another to satellites. Many markets are getting subscription TV services. Usually, these offer movies and occasional sports or other special events. The picture is not delivered to the subscriber's set by cable; rather, it is bounced off a satellite and picked up by a decoding device in each home. Home video uses are progressing beyond games.

RCA lost millions trying to sell consumers on videodisc systems, but it has not given up. Videodiscs, unlike video-cassettes, cannot record off the air. Although a federal Court of Appeals in 1981 ruled that the pirating of copyrighted material from the air was illegal, there was no effective means of enforcing the decision on existing sets. Because a prerecorded videocassette of a feature motion picture cost $50 to $80, most owners of videocassette equipment either taped them off the air or rented a cassette. One Manhattan store stocked 5000 rental titles, and the usual price was about what a couple would spend for tickets.

Low-power television may or may not offer a major break-through. When announced, there was such a rush of applications for the low-cost, low-power transmission frequencies (which typically would reach no more than 20 miles), that the FCC froze applications. By then there were 7000 on file. Congress rejected allocation by lottery and insisted on comparative hearings where there were competing applicants for the same frequencies. This promised to delay introduction of LPTV into urban areas for several years, although it might be established quickly in rural sections. Although there was language in the Congressional authorization bill of 1982 about favoring applications from minority and other disadvantaged groups, it remains to be seen just what that would mean. The bill contains no limitations on the number of frequencies that a given owner could operate, and the commercial viability of LPTV rests almost certainly on some sort of interconnection through satellites. Still, LPTV does offer some hope for specialized programming, often likened to that from a specialized magazine.

What emerges is a picture of a federal regulatory commission, the FCC, that has a long history of trying to regulate as little as possible, and which in turn is under the watchful eye of a Congress that is highly sensitive about the few attempts at boldness that the agency has shown. In the 1980s, in keeping with the general deregulatory mood, the commision is giving up most of its pretense about setting standards for cable or even over-the-air broadcasters. It has more than its limited staff and resources can hope to do in keeping some sort of reins on the common carriers. The most notable of these is American Telephone & Telegraph, the largest corporation in the world, which dominates not only the American telephone industry but is deeply involved in most related message delivery systems as well. In a dramatic development in 1982, the Justice Department concluded its years of negotiations with AT&T, agreeing to drop its antitrust actions in return for breaking the firm into several independent subsidiaries and for getting out of some aspects of the communication business. No one is sure of the long-term ramifications of this development. The FCC is certain to have its hands full with that one for a long time.

# 9

## HOW DO WE PRESERVE
## FREE EXPRESSION?

**Freedom of expression is not a doctrine; it is a process. Its strength is not in its careful definition, but in its liberal interpretation.**

It should be clear by now that it does not matter what the Founding Fathers meant by freedom of expression. What matters is how each generation takes those words in the First Amendment, reinterprets them in light of its own needs, and applies their spirit.

If we could divine their intended meaning (and there were many, often contradictory, meanings), we would not know much. The most accurate model of knowledge is not, after all, memorizing the multiplication table, something that once learned is settled, dependable, and unchanging. A more generalizable model was suggested by Mark Twain, who noted that in his days as an apprentice river boat pilot, he memorized every bend and shoal on the Mississippi River, only to find that because the river kept changing, he had to learn them over and over again. What he really had learned, of course, was how to apply facts he had learned to changing conditions. So must we all.

A certain part of all of us longs for certainty, often promised in shibboleths such as, "This is a nation of laws, not of men." Certainly, as the saying suggests, there is a continuity of values from generation to generation; however, this is essentially a nation of flesh-and-blood men and women. They frame, interpret, and enforce the laws in their own ways, unlike earlier generations and unlike their successors.

It is virtually impossible to write an unambiguous sentence. Certainly, "Congress shall make no law . . . abridging freedom of speech or of the press" means both more and less than what it says. What it states is a commitment to giving the benefit of the doubt to issues of free expression when weighing them against other societal interests. It is not a prescription; it is not even a yardstick. It is an ideal.

We have seen how procedural safeguards are of little value in times of crisis. The courts, although far from a perfect guardian for the long-range public good against temporary spasms of nationalism or other hysteria, are the best institution we have for that purpose. If, as attorneys are fond of saying, "hard cases make bad law," it is also true that hard cases force fundamental choices. It is in such decisions that society, through its courts, bites the bullet and spells out what is *really* important. Sometimes, looking backward, those decisions look foolish, but that is imposing an unfair standard on those who had to answer real questions at that moment. One of the beauties of a judicial system rooted in the pragmatism of common law is that if those same questions are raised in another time, in another set of circumstances, the answer can be different.

Men and women who have been at the center of important free expression battles are, for the most part, a scruffy lot. If you do not long to take these people home for dinner, at least thank them for their fanaticism and tenacity. Most of us shirk from testing values and laws; they did not.

Tolerance for those we most despise is the true test of freedom. It is a far better and more reliable guarantee of freedom than are brotherhood or even virtue. A person may love his brother so much that he feels himself appointed his keeper. Tolerance, by contrast, is based on mutual respect, not on an inferior-superior relationship. Virtue is not suspect because it is virtuous; rather, it is suspect because it can be invoked for any reason at all. Hitler and Stalin considered themselves the most virtuous of men. Probably no army in the history of the world has marched off without being convinced that it had virtue on its side.

Dogmas of whatever kind make toleration, and with it the pragmatic key of compromise, impossible. Dogma is the enemy of freedom. Freedom of speech could not become a civil liberty until most people in a society were willing to assume that a man's opinions, and particularly his religious opinions, were relative rather than uncompromising. Until contending political groups are willing to assume that their replacement by their opponents will not imperil the entire system, there can be no meaningful political freedom in a society.

One of the most distinguished of American jurists, Learned Hand, looked back on his long career and concluded that freedom of the press was less a legal concept than it was an "admonition of moderation." The First Amendment did not really mean *no* law; it meant that any such law must be "the result of an honest effort to embody a compromise or adjustment." The pragmatic nature of common law insists on this approach.

For obvious reasons, we have quoted many legal authorities throughout this book. They usually formulate the issues and society's tentative answers to them, but it is the general public that must make them meaningful. For that reason, it seems appropriate to end on a quotation from a popular observer of the scene, a man who has drawn cartoons, written novels, and produced plays that explore the foibles of twentieth-century life. Jules Feiffer (1978) put it this way:

> Our national affinity for powerlessness makes us yearn for a return to the good old days of capital punishment, for getting even. And why not? I've often yearned for it myself—thirty or forty times a day. Not in the case of convicted murderers or terrorists, people like that. I yearn for it in the case of theater critics, my book publisher, my landlord, Con Edison, taxi drivers, motorcycle thugs who wear swastikas, any teen-ager on a city bus playing a transistor radio. If there existed such a thing as justice in this country, no one would be going around free who disagreed with me, displeased me, or who hurt my feelings. But we do not have justice. All we have is law, and the law tells me that I cannot sentence people to death on a whim, or close down their businesses on a whim, or blacklist them from their jobs on a whim.

Freedom is neither free nor static. Like a farm, freedom requires constant attention and hard work. The person who inherits a farm may get one fine harvest, based on the work of his predecessor, but he will have to plow, sow, fertilize, and tend each new crop. Crops do not just happen and freedom does not just stay free. As there are thieves, weeds, and insects to keep out of fields, so are there enemies of freedom as well. Of these, dogmas and intolerance are the most dangerous.

# REFERENCES

## CHAPTER 1

ABRAHAM, H. J. (1968) The Judicial Process. New York: Oxford University Press.
Commission on Freedom of the Press (1947) A Free and Responsible Press. Chicago: University of Chicago Press.
DENNISTON, L. (1981) Conference Presentation. Athens, Georgia (April).
HAND, L. (1953) The Spirit of Liberty. New York: Knopf.
HOLMES, O. W., Jr. (1881) The Common Law. Boston: Little, Brown.
KRISLOV, S. (1968) The Supreme Court and Political Freedom. New York: The Free Press.
Royal Commission of Newspapers (1981) Final Report. Ottawa: Information Canada.
SIEBERT, F., T. PETERSON, and W. SCHRAMM (1963) Four Theories of the Press. Champaign: University of Illinois Press.

## CHAPTER 2

ALEXANDER, J. (1963) in S. N. Katz (ed.) A Brief Narrative of the Case and Trial of John Peter Zenger. Cambridge, MA: Harvard University Press.
BURY, J. B. (1913) A History of Freedom of Thought. New York: Henry Holt.
CHAFEE, Z., Jr. (1941) Free Speech in the United States. Chicago: University of Chicago Press.
EISENSTEIN, E. (1978) The Printing Press as an Agent of Change. New York: Cambridge University Press.
LANGFORD, J. J. (1966) Galileo, Science and the Church. Ann Arbor: University of Michigan Press.
LEVY, L. W. (1960) Legacy of Suppression. Cambridge: Harvard University Press.
LINDE, H. A. (1981) "Courts and censorship." Minnesota Law Review 66 (November): 171-208.
MEIKLEJOHN, A. (1948) Free Speech and Its Relation to Self-Government. New York: Harper & Brothers.
SCHLESINGER, A. M. (1955) "Political mobs and the American Revolution, 1765-1776." Proceedings of American Philosophical Society 99: 244-250.
SCHOFIELD, H. (1915) "Freedom of the press in the United States." Publications of the American Sociological Society 9: 67-81.

SMITH, J. M. (1956) Freedom's Fetters. Ithaca, NY: Cornell University Press.
STEVENS, J. D. (1966) "Congressional history of the 1798 Sedition Law." Journalism
    Quarterly 43 (Summer): 247-256.


CHAPTER 3


BRAESTRUP, P. (1977) Big Story. Boulder, CO: Westview Press.
CHAFEE, Z., Jr. (1941) Free Speech in the United States. Chicago: University of
    Chicago Press.
EMERSON, T. I. (1970) The System of Free Expression. New York: Random House.
HIGHAM, J. (1965) Strangers in the Land. New Brunswick: Rutgers University Press.
KNIGHTLY, P. (1975) The First Casualty. New York: Harcourt Brace Jovanovich.
MURPHY, P. L. (1979) World War I and the Origin of Civil Liberties in the United
    States. New York: W. W. Norton.
NELSON, H. L. (1967) Freedom of the Press From Hamilton to the Warren Court.
    Indianapolis: Bobbs, Merrill.
ROCHE, J. P. (1963) The Quest for the Dream. New York: Macmillan.
STEVENS, J. D. (1969) "Press and community toleration: Wisconsin in World War I."
    Journalism Quarterly 46 (Summer): 255-259.


CHAPTER 4


BOORSTIN, D. J. (1953) The Genius of American Politics. Chicago: University of
    Chicago Press.
COLE, M. (1955) Jehovah's Witnesses. New York: Vanity Press.
GREEN, J. R. (1942) "Liberty under the Fourteenth Amendment: 1942-1943," Wash-
    ington University Law Review 28 (Summer): 251-271.
HAMLIN, D. (1980) The Nazi-Skokie Conflict. Boston: Beacon Books.
KIM, R. C. (1964) "The Constitutional legacy of the Jehovah's Witnesses." Southwest
    Social Science Quarterly (September): 125-134.
LENS, S. (1964) The Futile Crusade. Chicago: Quadrangle Books.
LIPSET, S. (1959) Political Man. New York: Doubleday.
MANWARING, D. R. (1962) Render Unto Caesar. Chicago: University of Chicago
    Press.
NEIER, A. (1979) Defending My Enemy. New York: Dutton.
PEMBER, D. R. (1969) "The Smith Act as a restraint on the press." Journalism Mono-
    graph 10 (May).
ROCHE, J. P. (1963) The Quest for the Dream. New York: Macmillan.
THOMAS, N. (1923) The Conscientious Objector in America. New York: B. W.
    Huebsch.
TRUEBLOOD, D. E. (1966) The People Called Quakers. New York: Harper & Row.


CHAPTER 5


BOWLES, D. (1977) "Newspaper support for free expression in times of alarm, 1920
    and 1940." Journalism Quarterly 54 (Summer): 271-279.
FRIENDLY F. W. (1981) Minnesota Rag. New York: Random House.
GLESSING, R. (1970) The Underground Press in America. Bloomington: Indiana
    University Press.

GRAHAM, F. P. (1972) Press Freedoms Under Pressure. New York: Twentieth Century Fund.

KNOLL, E. (1981) "National security: the ultimate threat to the First Amendment." Minnesota Law Review 66 (November): 161-170.

LOFTON, J. (1981) The Press as Guardian of the First Amendment. Columbia, SC: University of South Carolina Press.

MORLAND, H. (1981) The Secret That Exploded. New York: Random House.

MURPHY, P. L. (1981) "Near v. Minnesota in the context of historical developments." Minnesota Law Review 66 (November): 95-160.

OAKES, J. L. (1982) "Prior restraint since the Pentagon Papers." Kenneth Murray Lecture, Ann Arbor, Michigan (March).

## CHAPTER 6

ANDISON, F. S. (1977) "TV violence and viewer aggression: a cumulation of study results." Public Opinion Quarterly 41 (Fall): 314-331.

BORHNSTEDT, G. W. et al. (1981) "Adult perspectives on children's autonomy." Public Opinion Quarterly 45 (Winter): 443-462.

COMSTOCK, A. (1967) in R. Bremner (ed.) Traps for the Young. Cambridge, MA: Belknap Press.

COMSTOCK, G. (1980) Television in America. Beverly Hills, CA: Sage Publications.

DORR, A. and P. KOVARIK (1980) "Some of the people some of the time—but which people?: televised violence and its effects," pp. 183-199 in E. L. Palmer and A. Dorr, Children and the Faces of Television. New York: Academic Press.

GOODMAN, P. (1960) Growing Up Absurd. New York: Random House.

KONVITZ, M. (1946) The Alien and Asiatic in American Law. Ithaca, NY: Cornell University Press.

LYLE, J. and H. HOFFMAN (1972) "Explorations in patterns of television viewing by pre-school-age children," in E. A. Rubinstein (ed.) Television and Social Behavior. Washington, DC: Government Printing Office.

MURRAY, R. K. (1955) Red Scare. Minneapolis: University of Minnesota Press.

National Commission on Obscenity and Pornography (1970) Final Report. New York: Random House.

O'BRYANT, S. L. and C. R. CORNER-BOLZ (1978) "Teaching 'the tube' with family teamwork." Children Today 7 (May/June): 21-25.

PRESTON, W. (1963) Aliens and Dissenters. New York: Harper & Brothers.

SINGER, J. L. and D. G. SINGER (1979) Paper at Broadcasting Symposium, Manchester, England (February).

STEVENS, J. D. (1971) "From behind barbed wire: freedom of the press in World War II Japanese centers." Journalism Quarterly 48 (Summer): 279-287.

TEN BROEK, J. et al. (1954) Prejudice, War and the Constitution. Berkeley: University of California Press.

## CHAPTER 7

CHAFEE, Z. (1947) Government and Mass Communication. Chicago: University of Chicago.

EISENSTEIN, E. (1978) The Printing Press as an Agent of Change. New York: Cambridge University Press.

EMERSON, T. I. (1970) The System of Free Expression. New York: Random House.
NIMMER, M. B. (1980) "Does copyright abridge the First Amendment guarantees of free speech and press?" UCLA Law Review 17 (June): 1180-1204.

CHAPTER 8

GILLMOR, D. M. (1966) Free Press and Fair Trial. Washington, DC: Public Affairs Press.
HEAD, S. W. and C. H. STERLING (1982) Broadcasting in America. Boston: Houghton Mifflin.
LOFTON, J. (1966) Justice and the Press. Boston: Beacon Press.
MILLER, A. R. (1971) The Assault on Privacy. Ann Arbor: University of Michigan Press.
PEMBER, D. R. (1972) Privacy and the Press. Seattle: University of Washington Press.
ROSEN, P. T. (1980) The Modern Stentors. Westport, CT: Greenwood Press.
TRAUB, J. (1981) "The nonstop news network." Columbia Journalism Review 20 (July/August): 58-61.
WARREN, S. and L. BRANDEIS (1890) "The right of privacy." Harvard Law Review 4 (December): 193-220.

CHAPTER 9

FEIFFER, J. (1978) "Love/hate and the First Amendment." The Nation 230 (July): 19-20.
HAND, L. (1953) The Spirit of Liberty. New York: Knopf.

# INDEX

# ABOUT THE AUTHOR

JOHN D. STEVENS has been Professor of Communication at the University of Michigan since 1967. His research and teaching have focused on the history and legal aspects of mass communication. A native of Indiana, where he worked on daily newspapers, he received his Ph.D. from the University of Wisconsin. He formerly taught at Wisconsin and Washington State Universities. This is his second Sage CommText. He was co-author of *Communication History* (1980), Volume 2 of the series. He also was co-author of *Mass Media and the National Experience* (1971) and *The Rest of the Elephant* (1973), as well as several book chapters, articles, and reviews in publications such as *Journalism Quarterly*, *Journalism History*, *Journal of Negro History*, *Journal of Popular Culture*, and *Columbia Journalism Review*.